When the Sun Rides High

Tell us a story
When the sun rides low,
Drawing the dark
Over all below.

Tell us a story
When the sun rides high,
Drawing the day
To the top of the sky.

Tell us a story
Of when and of why,
When the sun rides low,
When the sun rides high.
~Dawn L. Watkins

Reading 2B   Second Edition

BJU PRESS
Greenville, South Carolina

NOTE:
The fact that materials produced by other publishers may be referred to in this volume does not constitute an endorsement of the content or theological position of materials produced by such publishers. Any references and ancillary materials are listed as an aid to the student or the teacher and in an attempt to maintain the accepted academic standards of the publishing industry.

READING 2-B, Second Edition
When the Sun Rides High

Produced in cooperation with the Bob Jones University School of Education and Bob Jones Elementary School.

© 1998, 2007 BJU Press
First edition © 1982
Greenville, South Carolina 29614

ISBN 978-1-59166-750-6

15   14   13   12   11   10   9   8   7   6   5   4   3   2   1

Contents

Coastal Lands

JOURNEY
B O O K S

Special Deeds

Making Melody

Acknowledgments

A careful effort has been made to trace the ownership of selections included in this textbook in order to secure permission to reprint copyright material and to make full acknowledgment of their use. If any error or omission has occurred, it is purely inadvertent and will be corrected in subsequent editions, provided written notification is made to the publisher.

Houghton Mifflin Company: Glossary material based on the lexical database of the *Children's Dictionary,* copyright © 1981 Houghton Mifflin Company. No part of this book may be reproduced or transmitted in any form or by any means, electronic or mechanical, including photocopying and recording, or by any information storage or retrieval system, except as may be expressly permitted by the 1976 Copyright Act or with prior written permission from both Houghton Mifflin Company and the Bob Jones University Press.

"Until I Saw the Sea," from *I Feel the Same Way* by Lilian Moore. Copyright © 1967, © renewed 1995 Lilian Moore Reavin. Used by permission of Marian Reiner for the author.

Photo Credits

The following agencies and individuals have furnished materials to meet the photographic needs of this textbook. We wish to express our gratitude to them for their important contribution.

Corel Corporation
Breck P. Kent
Naval Photographic Center, Washington, D.C.
Photo Disc, Inc.
Wright State University

A Tide Pool
Photo Disc Inc. 31; Breck P. Kent 30, 32, 33, 35 (both); Corel Corporation 34

Until I Saw the Sea
Naval Photographic Center, Naval District, Washington, D.C. 89

The Wright Flyer
Archives & Special Collections, University Library, Wright State University 179, 180

Coastal Lands

Hurricane!

Karen Wooster

illustrated by Sherry Neidigh

Storm's Coming

Shanda and Travis splashed from puddle to puddle outside their house. Travis made very big splashes. Shanda squealed as water flew everywhere.

"Storm's coming! Storm's coming!" Shanda chanted with each splash.

Mama stood in the doorway. "Shanda, Travis."

The two children raced to the porch. They took off their soaking wet raincoats and boots. Inside, the house was cool. Shanda shook her damp curls and shivered.

"Travis, please turn on the radio," said Mama. "We need to find out where the storm is now."

In the middle of a program, a man began to speak. "We interrupt this program for the latest news. The storm off the coast has been upgraded to a hurricane. It is moving toward the north, northwest. Keep your radio on for further news."

"Will we have to go to a shelter this time?" Travis kept his eyes on Mama's face.

"I don't know yet." Mama rested her hand on his head. "We will keep the radio on. Your dad will be home soon. He and I will decide what to do." She patted his arm. "The Lord will take care of us."

The kitchen door slammed. Daddy stepped inside the kitchen. His hair was wet. Raindrops ran in little rivers down his face and neck.

"Daddy," said Travis. "Did you hear the news? A hurricane is coming!"

Daddy wiped his feet on the mat. "Yes, Travis," he said. "I heard the news on the car radio. I got home as soon as I could. Let me talk to Mama."

"What can I do, Daddy?" asked Travis.

"You can pick up everything in the yard that the wind could blow away. Put everything in the shed. Shanda can help you."

Shanda and Travis hurried to help. Travis carried the trash cans to the shed. Shanda splashed behind him, carrying a lawn chair. At every step, she chanted, "Storm's coming!"

When nothing was left to put away, they looked for Daddy. He was on the other side of the house, taping the windows. "Why do you always put tape on the windows before a storm, Daddy?" asked Shanda.

"Tape keeps the glass from flying everywhere if the window cracks." Daddy tossed a roll of tape to Travis. "If you will finish taping the outside, I will tape the inside of the windows."

"Okay, Daddy." Travis grinned.

5

Shanda went inside with Daddy. Mama looked up.

"We have plenty of food," she said. "There are still lots of batteries for the flashlight and the radio. I don't think we need anything from the store."

When all the work was finished, everyone gathered in the kitchen. It was late by the time they sat down for supper. During supper the wind began to blow harder. Shanda and Travis stared out the window. Broken branches blew across the yard.

The Storm

"I'm glad we picked everything up," said
Travis.

Daddy turned the radio up louder. "Winds
from the hurricane are now reaching the coast,"
said the announcer. "The hurricane is a category
four, but it has not turned toward land. There is
no need to go to a shelter at this time. However,
we can expect high winds and heavy rain. Please
keep your radio on."

After supper Mama rolled out sleeping bags. "You may sleep down here tonight," she said.

Shanda and Travis hurried through their baths. Soon they were tucked into the warm sleeping bags. After praying, Mama sang to them softly. They fell asleep to the sound of rain drumming on the windows.

Before dawn the wind began howling. The noise woke Shanda, and she stared into the dark. She got up and went to the kitchen where Mama and Daddy were sitting.

"The wind is really loud," she said. "It sounds like a sad lady moaning."

"Maybe it's looking for something to eat like I am," said Travis from behind her.

"You and Shanda run upstairs and get dressed," said Mama. "We will eat early this morning since Travis is so hungry."

Bacon was sizzling in the pan when Shanda
and Travis sat down at the table.

"Mmm," said Travis.

While everyone was eating, the lights flickered
and went out. Shanda dropped her fork with a
clatter. "Stay still while I light the candles," said
Daddy. Soon bright flames glowed in the dim
light. Daddy turned up the radio.

"The hurricane is moving up the coast at fifteen
miles an hour," said the announcer. "You are
advised to stay inside. Keep your radio on for
more updates."

"Since the power is off, the stove won't work," said Mama.

"I'm glad we got to eat," said Travis. "Is this what it was like when you were a boy?"

"No." Daddy laughed. "It's more like when my grandfather was a boy. People really lived without electric lights, radio, and the telephone."

Mama carried the candles to the living room. Shanda curled up on Mama's lap. Travis sat quietly by Daddy's feet. Daddy told them a story he had been told when he was growing up.

The wind began to howl and blow even louder. "Now the wind is roaring like a lion," whispered Shanda.

"Like a hungry lion!" teased Travis.

"Let's sing some songs," said Daddy. "Then the wind won't seem so loud to you."

They sang song after song. Suddenly they heard a crash! Shanda clutched her mother. Travis sat up. "What was that?" he asked.

Daddy went to the window. "Just a tree falling," he said.

"Will a tree fall on our house?" asked Shanda.

Daddy smiled a little. "I hope not."

They all sat still for a time. Shadows from the candlelight flickered on the walls.

Daddy's voice sounded loud and strong when he spoke. "Let's pray again and ask God to give us courage."

"Dear Lord," he prayed, "You promised to be with us always. Help us not to be afraid. Teach us to trust You. In Jesus' name. Amen."

Discovery

"Now it's Mama's turn to tell a story," said Daddy.

Mama smiled. "What story would you like to hear?"

"David and the giant," said Travis.

"Yes, David and the giant," said Shanda.

Mama began to speak, and they forgot about the wind. At last the story was finished. Mama set a tray on the table. There were sandwiches, pears, and four glasses of milk.

spear

"The wind isn't as loud," said Travis.

"Is the storm over?" asked Shanda.

"Not yet," said Daddy. "It's still raining. But it looks like the hurricane missed us. Listen."

"The hurricane is now headed out to sea," said the radio announcer.

"Hooray!" cried the children.

Mama laughed. "Since you have to stay inside, why don't you draw pictures for a while?"

Late in the afternoon the rain slowed down to a drizzle. Everyone put on raincoats and boots. They went outside to explore.

"Everything looks different," said Travis.

Shanda sniffed the air. "It smells different too. Clean and fresh."

She pointed to the yard. "Look! There is the tree the wind blew over!" She ran to the fallen tree. "I can climb a tree now," she said with a giggle.

Shanda walked up and down the tree trunk. Travis explored the roots. He poked at the little bugs scurrying up and down.

"Come down here," called Mama from the beach. The children scrambled down to join her and Daddy.

The beach was covered with shells and seaweed.

"They were swept up by the waves," said Mama. "Look!" A rainbow-colored jellyfish lay on the wet sand.

"And a big wooden plank!" cried Travis. "Do you think it came from an old wrecked ship?"

"Maybe." Daddy smiled.

The family spent the rest of the afternoon on the beach, collecting treasures from the sea. They watched the big waves that still pounded along the shore. At last they climbed the path to the house.

"I'm glad the storm is over," said Travis. "But it was a safe feeling to stay together inside the house."

"Storms make us depend more on the Lord," Daddy said. "Maybe that is why He sends them."

Shanda splashed on the path. "God loves us!" she sang. "God loves us! He sends big storms, but He loves us!"

Sea Island Mystery

Wendy M. Harris

illustrated by Kathy Pflug

Lady's Island

"Did you look out your window yet?" asked Lena. "Spanish moss is dripping off the trees. Can you smell the salt water?"

"Spending summer on an island is going to be great! But I am going to miss Mom and Dad," said Marcus.

"I hope Grandma gets better soon," said Lena.

"Me too," said Marcus. He glanced out the window. "Look, there are the ponies! I can't wait to ride."

Lena said, "They look calm, but I don't want to ride them."

"Not all ponies are like Sugar Foot, Lena. Come on, everyone else is in the kitchen."

Aunt Fran slid another slice of peach pie on the children's plates. "Do you want anything else?"

"No, thank you. I'm stuffed!" said Lena.

"Milk, please," said Marcus. He grinned. "I want to know all about this place. It's so close to the ocean that there have to be stories of shipwrecks and pirate treasure! Tell us everything!"

Uncle Vance laughed. "Well, there isn't much to tell. There were lots of shipwrecks off the coast. But other islands are closer to the wrecks.

"It's more likely that pirates chose those islands to hide treasure on. You will have to be happy with exploring Lady's Island and riding the ponies this summer."

woah

Lena smiled weakly at Marcus. He winked at her.

"Wait, Vance," said Aunt Fran. "What about the church mystery? Isn't there treasure in that story?"

"Tell us, tell us!" said Marcus.

"You should visit Miss Shank," said Aunt Fran. "She knows more about this story than anyone."

"Yes, and try digging for the treasure too," said Uncle Vance. "The church burned down a hundred years ago, and the ruins are just a mile away. You can explore there all you want."

"Wow, a real mystery!" said Lena.

"And what a summer we're going to have!" said Marcus.

Lady's Island Secret

In the mornings, Marcus and Lena fed and groomed the ponies. In the afternoons they explored Lady's Island and the crumbled ruins of the church. They were looking for the church treasure. They didn't find it.

They did find long-legged birds in the marsh and crabs that ran sideways on the beach. With Marcus's help, Lena started riding a gentle pony. But she would go only as fast as a walk.

After a few days, Marcus and Lena went to see Miss Shank.

"Come on, Lena. Let's trot. We can get there faster," said Marcus.

"No," she said. "I like walking."

The heat of the day steamed Marcus, Lena, and the ponies. Only a small sea breeze rippled through the Spanish moss. Lena could feel the sweat from her pony. She sniffed. Hot pony was a nice smell.

They tied the ponies to a tree in the shade and walked up to the big house. A lady answered the door. "You must be Lena and Marcus, right? Your Aunt Fran told me I would be getting a visit from you two." Miss Shank asked them to sit in the porch swing, and she brought out dishes of cool banana pudding.

"Thank you!" said Marcus and Lena together.

They had just taken a bite when Marcus said, "What can you tell us about the missing treasure?"

Lena said, "Marcus!"

Miss Shank laughed. "Fran told me you wanted to know about the treasure. Well, it was my great-great-great- . . . oh, I forget how many greats, but Gussy was one of those great-grandmothers. She was just a girl the night the Spanish attacked.

"She heard her father, the preacher, tell Able Fuller to hide the treasure.

"There were silver candlesticks and offering plates and such. The church was not all built yet, but there were these treasures."

"Ooo," said Lena.

"Gussy said she saw Able ride off with the treasure toward the church. The Spanish troops raided her house soon after Able left. Able and the treasure were never seen again. Some people said he had run off with it."

"Did he?" asked Marcus.

"Gussy said there was never a more trusted man than Able Fuller. Years later the story was told that Able was sent to jail in Spain. They said he was an old man before he got out. Gussy said she thought Able may have hidden the treasure before the Spanish troops got him. If that's true, the treasure is still on this island."

Lena said, "I felt chills run down my back."

When they walked back to the ponies, Marcus said, "We're going to find that treasure."

Lena's pony nuzzled her arm and blew its warm breath into her hand. She smiled at it and petted its velvet nose.

Lady's Island Dig

"If I were Able Fuller, where would I hide treasure?" Marcus leaned on his spade. Lena sat down next to him.

"We've dug all around this church! It just isn't here! I think Able did run off with the treasure," said Lena.

"No, he didn't, Lena. He was a good man. Now think! Where would you hide it?"

"All right, all right. Let me think . . . again." Lena flopped onto her side. The two thought for a while. "Oh!" said Lena.

"Did you think of something?" asked Marcus.

"No, I'm getting ants in my hair." Lena stood up and shook her head.

Marcus stood staring at all the places where they had dug. "If Spanish troops came, they would have seen fresh dirt and known that Able had been digging. They would have found the treasure."

Lena said, "Maybe they didn't see the fresh dirt."

Marcus said, "But why wouldn't they have seen it?"

"Maybe it wasn't here," said Lena.

Marcus looked around. Across the road was a graveyard. Then he turned back to Lena, his eyes wide. "They wouldn't think fresh dirt in a graveyard was odd! The treasure must be hidden there!" Marcus raced across the road. Lena was right behind him. They read names and dates from the gravestones. Marcus held his spade ready.

"Marcus, we can't dig here! It isn't right! I won't let you do this!"

"I'm not going to, Lena. Look at the dates. These graves aren't old enough anyway."

"Oh Marcus! You scared me! Let's go home." Lena turned back to look at the church ruins. She thought. "Marcus, did Miss Shank say that the people were just putting the church up when the Spanish marched through?"

"Yes, it was still being worked on. Why?" asked Marcus.

"Wouldn't there be fresh dirt around the church?" she asked. "You know, from people working on the church."

"Yes, but we've dug all around the church and didn't find anything."

Lena looked at Marcus. "But we haven't dug inside the church. What if the floor had not been put in yet?"

Marcus looked at Lena. The two ran back across the road and into the church. They dug without saying a word. They came back every day and worked.

On the fourth day, the spade hit something hard. Marcus and Lena dropped to their knees and scooped dirt from around a box. It looked old, very old.

"Oh Marcus," whispered Lena, "we found it."

Marcus lifted the lid and looked inside. Lena could see only a little glint of silver.

"We're going to need help," said Marcus.

"I'll go get Uncle Vance," said Lena.

"You have to go fast. I can go if you don't want to."

"No," said Lena. "I can do it." She mounted her pony and galloped away.

A Tide Pool

Karen Wooster and Eileen M. Berry

During the night the tide came in. Seawater crashed over the rocks. Waves rippled farther and farther up the beach. At last they spread their lacy foam to the high-water mark. Then slowly, slowly, the water returned to the sea.

Not all the water went back out with the tide. Some water was caught in deep holes between the rocks. This trapped water is called a *tide pool*.

Each day the tide brings fresh seawater into the pools. The small sea animals that live in the pools get their food from the seawater. God has given each of these sea animals special ways to survive.

A sea anemone takes different shapes. When it is in danger, it pulls in its little tentacles. Then it looks a bit like an old, wrinkled orange. But when the danger is gone, the sea anemone opens up. Then it looks like a beautiful flower.

God made these tentacles to help feed the sea anemone. The tentacles wave back and forth in the water. They sting small animals that come too close. These animals will be the sea anemone's next meal.

Another animal in the tide pool is the sea urchin. During the tides, it clings to the rocks with tiny tube feet that keep it from being swept away. When the water is still, the sea urchin moves slowly along the bottom of the pool.

When the sea urchin is in danger, it hides between the rocks. But it does not really have to fear its enemies. It has so many spikes that it looks like a prickly pincushion.

The five arms of the starfish sometimes make it look like a fallen star lying in the tide pool. Along its arms are many tiny suckerlike feet. Water helps the feet of the starfish stick tightly to the rocks. If a starfish breaks off an arm, a new arm grows in place of the old one.

The clam lives inside a beautiful, closed shell.
When the tide comes into the pool, the clam opens
its shell to take in seawater. It eats tiny plants
from the water. Then it spits the water back out.

The clam has a single foot that it uses to move
itself in mud or sand.

The crab is a sea animal that swims in tide pools, but it also runs along the beach. It has eight legs for walking and swimming and two pincers that it uses as hands. With its pincers the crab can pick up its food.

God has given the crab a hard shell to keep it from being hurt. Some crabs live in the empty shells that other animals have left behind.

Each animal that shares the tide pool belongs to God. Big and small, funny-looking and beautiful, God cares for them all.

The Cranky Blue Crab

Dawn L. Watkins / illustrated by Tim Davis

And Out on Green Grass

Down by the sea
By its rippling edge,
Lived Crusty the Crab
Under Jaggedy Ledge.

Every ship that he saw
From the crest of a wave
Looked better to him
Than his water-worn cave.

When the sun shone too hot
On his back, he complained,
But he never was pleased
Whenever it rained.

One day the tide
Was at a new low;
Crusty said to the squid,
"I really should go.

"I'm bored with this place
And its limited range.
I think I'll live out
On the land for a change."

"But why," said the squid,
"Why make all this fuss?
The sea's the best home
For creatures like us."

"Maybe for you—
Not me," said the crab;
"Life in this cave
Is unbearably drab."

The tide rolled him out
On a wide sandy shore
With an ungentle push
And an unfriendly roar.

He climbed over beams
Of small rotting hulls.
Whenever he rested,
He was swooped by the gulls.

They dived for his shell;
They skimmed past his eyes.
"Look, look," they all cried,
"What a tasty surprise!"

Crusty shook a blue claw
As a threat most absurd.
"Stay out of my way,
You cantankerous birds!"

At the top of the ridge
Crusty met his first flea.
"And who," said the crab,
"Might this creature be?"

The flea tipped his head,
Tapped one of his feet—
"I'm the cleverest flea
That you'll ever meet."

The flea looked him over,
Then said with a grin—
"From the looks of you, sir,
We just might be kin."

Crusty thought this unlikely,
But he let it pass.
He went over the ridge
And out on green grass.

Behind him came Flea
In a leap and a bound.
"If you're new in these parts,
Let me show you around."

"Very well," said the crab,
"But don't slow me down.
I'm on an adventure."
And he frowned a crab frown.

"Do you have a name?"
Asked Crusty quite coolly.
Said the flea with a flourish,
" 'Tis Fleabus O'Tooly."

One Huzbumbley Crew

So off the two went
Away from sea's edge,
Across a wide meadow
Toward a dark hedge.

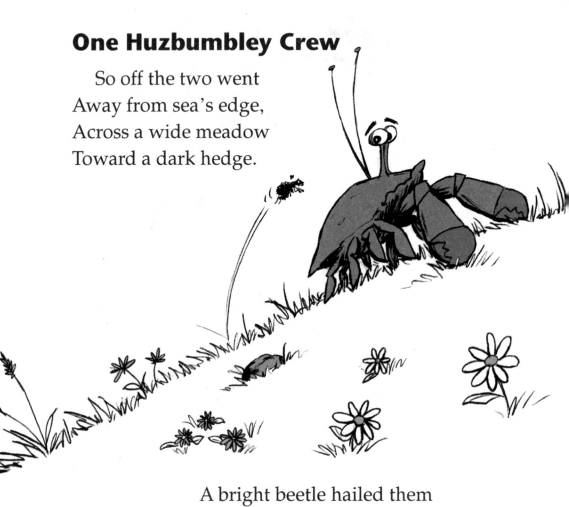

A bright beetle hailed them
As they went along.
"Hello, my friend Flea,
Want to hear a new song?"

"Who is this?" asked the crab,
His antennae knit.
"I don't want to stop here,
Not one little bit!"

"Oh, Beetle's all right,"
Said Flea with a smile.
"And it might do you good
To rest for a while."

The crab didn't like it,
But they stopped for a visit.
"This song," asked the Flea,
"What kind of song is it?"

"A song of the meadow,"
Said Beetle with pleasure.
"I wrote it myself.
Let me sing the first measure."

Beetle thrummed his hard wings,
With snib-ticklety-click.
"This," said the crab,
"Is no song. It's a trick!"

"Shhhh," warned the flea,
"Can't you be more polite?
What kind of a song
Did you ever write?"

Crusty said, "Ump harumph.
When I'm falling asleep,
I have often heard whales
Singing songs of the deep."

"Well, this is the meadow,
And the way Beetle sings
Is the way that we like it—
You remember these things."

Then Crusty was quiet
'Til the music was done.
"That was all very nice,
But I really must run."

"Where are you going?"
Asked Beetle Brightknee.
"I might go along
If you all would invite me."

Across the rich meadow
Came a winging of color;
So bright was the creature
It made flowers seem duller.

It settled at last
On a thistle near Crusty;
Its wings were deep purple,
And just slightly dusty.

"Hi, Flutterby,"
Said Beetle Brightknee.
"Good day to you, Wings,"
Said the good-natured flea.

"Hello," said the purple
And gold bedecked thing,
And ever so gracefully
Dipped her one wing.

It occurred to the crab
That he'd like to bow,
And then he remembered
He'd never learned how.

"This is a crab,"
Flea told Flutterby.
"He's on an adventure,
But didn't say why."

Flutterby said
In a voice like a song,
"He doesn't have to.
May I come along?"

"Yes, yes," said the beetle.
"Please do," said the flea.
Crusty smiled his first smile
Since he'd left the sea.

Three of them walked,
And one of them flew;
Together they made
One huzbumbley crew.

Until Gathering Dark

When they got near the hedge,
They heard a low buzz;
Crusty had no idea
Of what the buzz was.

Down on the crab zoomed
A huge swarm of bees
And set him to knocking
All eight of his knees.

"Oh, wait," said Flutterby,
"Please wait, if you will."
At the sound of her voice,
The bees hovered still.

"This is no flower
Though the colors seem right.
This crab is our guest—
And you gave him a fright."

When they heard Flutterby,
The bees backed away;
You may always believe
What the butterflies say.

48

"That was close," said the beetle.
"Sure was," said the flea.
"Oh, pah," said the crab,
"They didn't scare me."

"Shall I call them back?"
The butterfly said.
"Oh, don't bother," said he,
"Let them go on ahead."

Flea winked at Beetle,
And Flutterby flitted.
Crusty thought no one saw
That he'd been outwitted.

On they all went,
With the day growing hot.
"Our terrain," said Crusty,
"Is not like you've got."

"This is Sea Meadow,"
Said Beetle Brightknee.
"Sand's better," said Crab,
"If you care to ask me."

"Nobody does," said Flea,
As he climbed up a stone.
With crossed claws said Crusty,
"I will go on alone!"

"Now, wait," said Flutterby.
"Go ahead," said the flea.
"It's not safe," said Beetle,
"For one from the sea."

"I'm going," said Crusty,
And left in a huff.
"Let him go," said the flea,
"I've quite had enough."

"Be kind," said Flutterby,
"Let's follow a while."
And she won the flea over
With her wonderful smile.

They followed the crab
Until gathering dark.
And then in the distance
They heard a sharp bark.

"It's the fox," said Flutterby;
"I remember his voice.
We must stay with Crusty.
Now we've really no choice."

Deep in the Thicket

Deep in the thicket
The crab and the fox
Were sitting and talking
On top of some rocks.

"So you're new around here,"
Said Finefur the Sly.
"I know a few things
You might like to try."

Quietly, quietly
Breathed Flutterby,
"I'm afraid it's the fox
Who has things to try."

"I'll show you the city,"
Said Fox with a wink,
"Where lights are like stars;
Where there's soda to drink;

"Where there's music and money,
And fountains of gold,
And more things to eat
Than you ever could hold."

Whispered Beetle to Flea,
"Yes, I've heard of that tour;
It's a trip down his throat,
You can be pretty sure."

"Let's go," said the crab,
"That city's for me.
No more dull life
At the edge of the sea."

"So you've come from Seashore;
You've come a long way."
"I've walked half a mile
Since early today."

"Where are my manners?"
Asked Fox, grinning wide.
"You go to sleep,
And I'll give you a ride."

Then in a flash
The fox made a leap
And snatched the crab up
In his gleaming white teeth.

"Avaunt!" cried Flea
Like a knight on a charger.
And he sailed against Fox
Who was ninety times larger.

He grabbed Fox's tail
And bit down like a vice.
Fox sprang off the ground
And rolled over twice.

He fell back to earth
And let out a wail.
Then he scrambled around
And went chasing his tail.

Crusty meanwhile,
On his back in the dirt,
Yelled, "What are you doing?
I might have been hurt!"

"That's right," whispered Beetle
As he pushed the crab over.
"Now come with us quick,
Back to Sea Meadow clover."

"I will not," said the crab.
"Get your feet off of me.
As I told you before,
I don't need you three."

The fox disappeared
After several more bites;
Experience taught him
Who wins in flea fights.

Said the crab with a glare,
"You've run off my guide.
I won't see the lights now
Without my free ride."

To the Sound of the Waves

"You do take the cake,"
Said the flea in disgust.
"If you weren't so stubborn
You'd know who to trust."

"I just thought," said the crab,
"It would be such a pity,
If I came all this way
And then missed the big city."

"There is no big city,"
Said Flutterby firmly.
And the tone of her voice
Made him feel rather wormly.

"Flea saved you," said Beetle,
"From a terrible ride.
Fox only takes riders
From out to inside!"

"And, too," said the flea,
"Since we're speaking of things—
Those bees would have had you
Had it not been for Wings."

Crusty was solemn,
And if they'd had a lamp,
The rest would have seen
That his eyes were quite damp.

Crusty stared at his toes
While a full minute passed.
"Well, it's true what you say,"
Said Crusty at last.

"I'm rude and ungrateful,
And cranky and proud."
He somehow felt better
To say it out loud.

"Forgive my behavior;
Can't I please make amends?
I think I know now
Who to call my true friends."

"Of course, we forgive you,"
Said the other three then.
Crusty might have felt warmer,
But he couldn't say when.

"You've all been so kind,
And your meadow is grand.
But the sea's more for me;
I'm not built for land."

"Well, then," said Beetle,
"We'll lead you back home
To the sound of the waves
And the spray of the foam."

And now when the tide
Thunders in every day,
Crusty always remarks
How he likes it that way.

And Flutterby, Fleabus,
And Beetle Brightknee
Come down every day
For a chat by the sea.

Now when Beetle plays music
The crab hums along
And Fleabus is learning
To sing a whale song.

And Crusty's at home
Under Jaggedy Ledge,
Down by the sea,
By its rippling edge.

Far away in the land of Holland, the tulips bloom in bright red, yellow, and orange colors. The dikes hold back the waves of the sea. And the blades of the windmills sing whoosh, whoosh, whoosh as they turn in the wind.

In that far land a tale is told about a boy named Jan who lived down by the dikes. His family owned a small farm along the high-walled dikes.

The Boy and the Dike

Karen Wilt / illustrated by Tim Davis

Jan often walked down the gravel road alongside the dike. It led to his grandmother's house. But that was a long walk away.

He called his grandmother Oma, as all good Dutch children do. And she told him long tales as all good Dutch grandmothers do. Her tales were about brave Dutchmen and the things they had done. They were about the dikes that kept the sea from flooding the farms.

Jan loved to listen to Oma's stories. He went to visit her often. One day Mother wrapped up a loaf of fresh brown bread for Jan to give to Oma. Soon he was on his way.

"You may stay overnight if Oma asks you to," Mother called.

Jan skipped happily along the road. His wooden shoes clicked and clacked on the gravel. He stamped along beside the dike while the waves smashed and thrashed on the other side.

Jan splashed through a puddle of water. Then he stopped. It had not rained today. Where could the water have come from? Then he saw a tiny trickle of water coming from the dike. He looked at the tall, thick dike. A tiny hole had begun to grow, and the seawater was seeping through it.

"Oh, no!" Jan cried. He knew the little trickle would soon become a flood.

He stuck a stick in it. The water pushed it out.

He stuck a rock in it. The water pushed that out too.

Jan could tell the hole was growing quickly. He put his finger in the stream of water. Ever so slowly it stopped.

Jan looked across the field. No houses were in sight. He looked down the road. No cart rumbled along this late in the day. In fact, the sun had begun to set.

"Help!" Jan called.

No one heard. Jan did not dare leave. The hole would grow, and seawater would flood all the land for miles. He could never run quickly enough to get help.

He leaned against the dike and waited. The sun set. Above him the stars came out and the moon lit up the fields. Hours passed. But no one came near.

Jan nibbled on Oma's bread. He remembered the stories she had told about strong men. They had carried huge rocks to make the dikes strong. They had built them to protect the land.

They had battled with the sea. Now Jan would fight too. His finger felt as cold as ice, but he would not let the sea win the battle.

At last the long night ended. The sky grew lighter and lighter. A horse pulling a little milk cart rumbled down the road. "Help!" Jan cried.

The milkman and his son stopped their cart and came running. "What is wrong?" they asked.

"There is a hole in the dike. Quick! Get the men in the village," Jan said.

The milkman left his son to help Jan. Then he galloped off. While he was gone, Jan and the milkman's son waited. They heard the birds wake up and start their singing. They saw the top of the sun peep over the edge of the fields far away.

Then Oma rode up in her rickety goat cart. The milkman had stopped to give her the news first. She had a soft, warm blanket to wrap around Jan.

At last the Dutchmen of the village came running to fix the dike. Jan's father and mother and his brothers and sisters came too.

Jan sat close beside Oma as they rode home. His eyes drooped with sleep.

"Jan," she whispered, "now I have a new tale to tell—about a brave Dutch boy and the dikes of Holland."

The Old Fisherman

Becky Davis / illustrated by Del Thompson

A Song on the Wind

The sun shone down on the gray-white sand and on Marty and Ben. Marty sat on her beach blanket reading a book. Ben was finishing his sandcastle.

"Look, Marty," he called to his older sister, "I built a castle with towers and everything. And it has that thing around it to hold the water and alligators, whatever you call it."

"A moat," said Marty. "Pretty nice castle, Ben. I hope the ocean doesn't carry it away."

"No, I made the castle too far up on the beach for that." Ben pushed a lump of sand into a spot that was starting to crumble. "The wind might wreck it, though. It's blowing pretty hard today."

The wind blew sounds all around. There were sounds of sea gulls crying. There were sounds of waves crashing on the sand. Then came another sound floating on the wind.

"Fish! Fish! Fish!
I'll grab myself a fish.
I'll cook it just the way I wish.
I'll serve it in a silver dish.
Fish! Fish! Fish!"

The singsong voice drifted over the rocks and sand dunes. "What's that?" Ben asked.

"It sounds like a fisherman," Marty replied. She put her book down. "Let's go see."

"I think the sound is coming from the other side of those rocks," said Marty.

They climbed up some rocks and peeked over the edge. An old man sat near the edge of the ocean. It looked as though he had some fish in a pile beside him. The two children were too far away to tell for sure. But they could still hear the singsong voice.

"Fish! Fish! Fish!
Just look at all my fish.
I'll give them to my wife to fry.
She'll bake them in a nice fish pie.
And I'll eat fish until I die.
Fish! Fish! Fish!"

"Fish pie!" said Marty.

Marty and Ben giggled.

"He sounds nice!" Ben said. "Let's go meet him."

"No, Ben," Marty said. "We aren't supposed to go near strangers without Daddy or Mother."

Ben nodded. Then they both climbed on top of the rocks. There they could lean against the rocks and listen.

Ben said softly, "Now he's singing a church song. You hear it?"

"Yes," Marty whispered back. " 'Amazing Grace.' "

"If he's singing a song from church, that means we can go down and talk to him," Ben said. "Come on!"

"No, Ben!" Marty grabbed her brother by the wrist. "We aren't supposed to go near a stranger alone. Not even if he has on a stovepipe hat and looks like Abraham Lincoln!"

Benjamin Christian

"Well, then, let's go see if Daddy can come with us. Don't you want to meet that old man too?"

Marty did. They scrambled down the rocks. They ran through the hot sand to their house. Mr. Billings was putting away his tools from work.

"Mother, Daddy!" they both cried together as they ran up the path.

Ben was first. "We found an old man on the beach who sings songs about fish and fish pie and church songs, and he looks really nice, and can we go meet him?"

"Now," their father said, chuckling, "let me get the story straight. Did you want to meet someone on the beach who sings fish songs and church songs?"

"Yes! Yes!" said the children.

It wasn't long at all before the three of them were walking through the sand. Mr. Billings walked in the middle with one child holding each hand. Both of them were pulling him to make him go faster.

"I hope he hasn't gone," Ben said.

"He hasn't," Marty said. "Listen, I hear him singing! Oh, I wish Mother hadn't gone shopping. I want her to meet him too."

The same voice still floated above the sound of the waves. It was singing "Jesus, Savior, Pilot Me."

"That sounds like a voice I've heard before," Mr. Billings said.

The waves crashed loudly on the beach. But the old man looked around even before they were near.

He wore
a red shirt
and faded old
blue jeans. The
fish he had been
singing about were in
a bucket beside him. But
now Ben and Marty also saw
his wrinkled skin, tanned a dark
brown from being in the sun.
He had white eyebrows and white hair tucked
under a white cap.

But what twinkly gray eyes peered out from
under those eyebrows!

"Sir," said Mr. Billings, "I'm Robert Billings. I remember you. You're Mr. Christian, aren't you?"

The old man nodded and smiled. He whipped off his white cap and bowed before his three visitors. "Benjamin Christian is my name. I was born a Christian twice, the first time sixty-seven years ago, and the second time forty-one years ago when I was saved." When he looked up, his eyes were twinkling more than ever.

"You have the same name I do!" Ben said. "Except I'm not Benjamin Christian; I'm Benjamin Billings."

"Benjamin is a fine name to have," Mr. Christian said. "A fine Bible name."

A Sailor's Testimony

"Children," Mr. Billings said, "Mr. Christian gave his testimony at church only a few weeks ago. He sang some songs for us too."

"I don't remember seeing him," said Ben.

"That's because we go to children's church, Ben," whispered Marty.

"Well, Mr. Christian," said Ben, "I was born seven years ago. But I was born a Christian two years ago."

"Glad to meet you, young Ben," said Mr. Christian.

"And I'm Marty. Won't you tell us your testimony now, since we missed it?"

77

"Why surely, young man and little lady. That is, if your daddy doesn't mind hearing it again."

"Not at all!" said their father.

Mr. Christian turned over an empty bucket for Marty to sit on. Ben plopped right down on the sand. The men sat on the rocks.

"The wind was whipping more wildly than this on that day when I left home forty-nine years ago," Mr. Christian said. "I was a wicked boy. I wanted to get away from home and my mother's teaching. She was a Christian—twice. I had never been born again, and I didn't want to be."

The waves rushed onto the shore and washed back.

"I left my village with all my things packed into a bag. I went to a seaport. Ships were docked all up and down the coast. People were everywhere trading and selling, talking loudly, so loudly you couldn't even hear the sea gull crying.

"I got on a ship that was going far away. That was just what I wanted to do. I became a sailor.

"Oh, little friends, I'm ashamed to say it. But I was the wildest and wickedest sailor on the ship. The other men sometimes made fun of me for my name.

" 'Benjamin Christian!' they would yell at me. 'You're the worst Christian I've ever seen!'

"That only made me want to be all the more wicked. I wanted to forget everything my mother had tried to teach me. Oh, what a sinner I was!"

Mr. Christian stopped, listening to the crashing waves. "For years I went on like this. Sometimes I remembered the verses my mother had taught me. But I always put them out of my mind. I wanted to run away from God.

"But thank the Lord, He loved me too much to let me run away from Him. One night there was a storm at sea. Have you ever been through a storm on the beach?" Mr. Christian looked at Ben and Marty.

"Oh, yes!" Marty said. "Storms are loud and awful. They scare me!"

"Well, little lady, a storm at sea would scare you ten times worse. The sky was black with thunderclouds. The waves crashed against the ship. They crashed so hard that we were afraid the ship would be broken to bits. Even the sailors who had been sailing the seas all their lives were afraid in this storm.

"During those dark hours it seemed as if I remembered all the bad things I had ever done. It seemed as if all the things my mother had taught me came back to my mind. For the first time in many years, I bowed my head and prayed. I prayed, 'Oh, Lord, I'm a worthless sinner and I know it. Please forgive me of my sins and save me. If You will keep me safe through this storm, I'll live the rest of my life for You.' "

Amazing Grace

Mr. Christian looked over at Ben and Marty as
he finished his story. "Do you know what
happened? God did forgive me of my sins and
save me. And He kept me safe through that storm.
And I did what I promised I would do. I obeyed
God. My life was never the same after that. The
other sailors saw that I had become a real
Christian, a Christian in life, not only in my name.
And some of them were saved too. I went home
to my mother to thank her for praying for me."

"That storm sounds exciting," said Ben. "But I'm glad I was never in a storm like that."

"Yes, you should be glad," Mr. Christian said. "And be glad you were saved when you were young. Now you can live your entire life for the Lord. You don't have to waste any of it."

"Would it be all right if we come to visit you sometimes when you are here on the beach?" Marty asked.

"Why, yes. In fact, I would like to have all of your family visit me in my home tomorrow. I'll show you some of the things I collected while I was a sailor."

"Oh, boy!" both children exclaimed. "May we, Daddy?"

Mr. Billings looked at his children and then at Mr. Christian. "That would be very nice."

"Will we get to have some fish pie?" Ben asked, grinning.

"Oh, so you heard my song, did you?" Mr. Christian's eyes twinkled merrily. "Why, I wouldn't ever let you leave my house without giving you some fish pie!"

He threw back his head and sang,

"Fish! Fish! Fish!
My wife will cook our fish.
A fishy pie, a fishy cake.
Just look at all the things she'll bake!
You'll get a fishy stomachache
From fish, fish, fish!"

Marty and Ben laughed at this new verse to the song. Mr. Billings chuckled too.

But then Mr. Christian's face got thoughtful. "Children," he said, "I'm glad you like that song. But I have a story to tell you about a sailor who was in a storm at sea just like the one I was in. He was saved too, just like me. His name was John Newton."

"John Newton," murmured Ben. "I don't think I've ever met him."

Mr. Christian smiled. "That's because he lived a long time ago, Son. But he wrote the beautiful words to a song that you may know. It has become a very special song to me because he was saved pretty much the same way I was. The name of the song is 'Amazing Grace.' "

" 'Amazing Grace'!" Marty exclaimed. "I heard you singing that a little while ago!"

"So did I," said Ben. "I think it's going to be my favorite song now too."

"I sing it to thank God for saving me," Mr. Christian said. He looked out far over the ocean to the place where the water meets the sky and began to sing. Then Ben joined him. And soon Marty and Mr. Billings were singing too. Even the sea gulls were quiet as the four voices were carried on the wind over the rocks and sand dunes.

"Amazing grace!
How sweet the sound,
That saved a wretch like me!
I once was lost,
But now am found,
Was blind, but now I see."

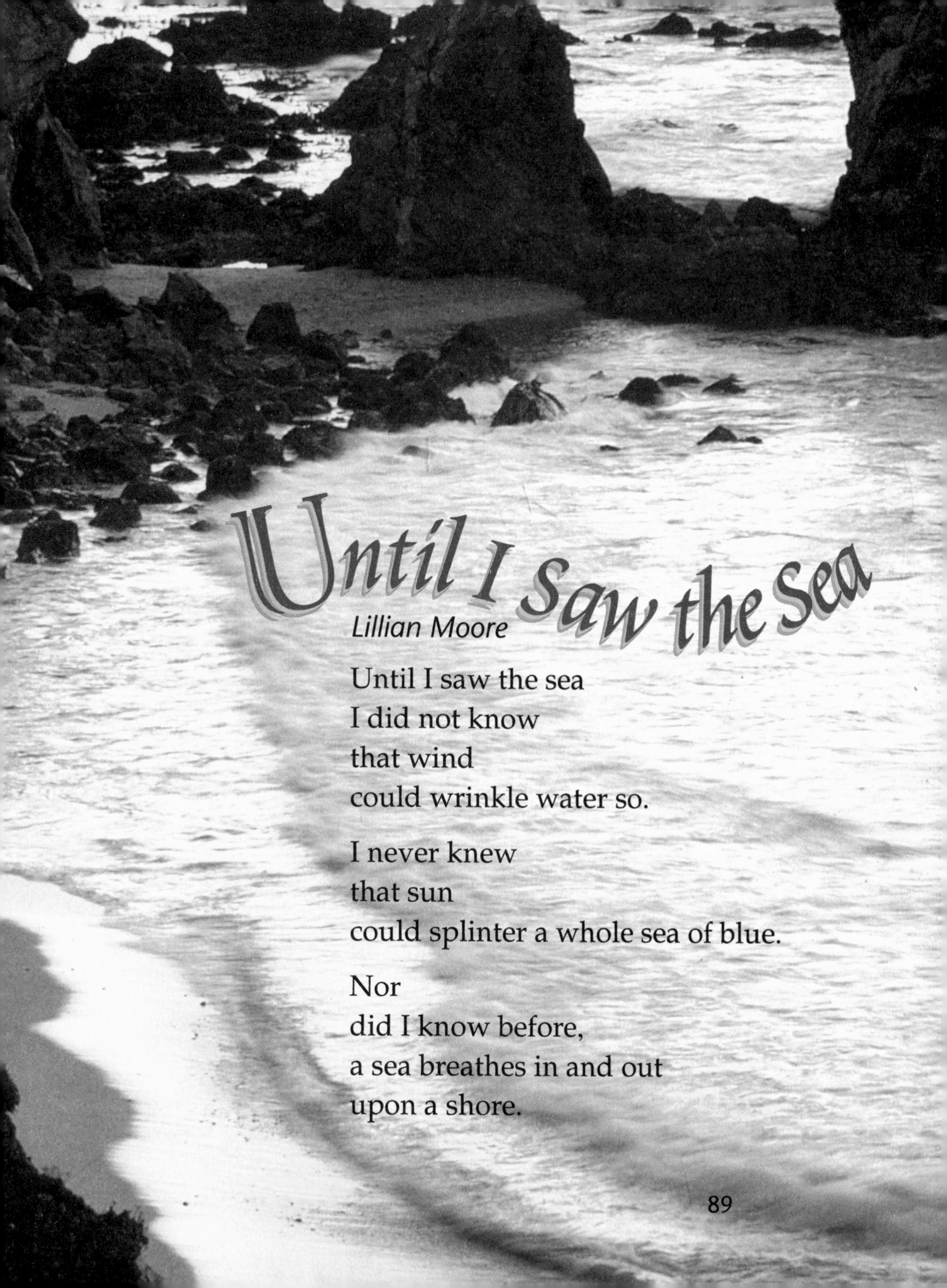

Until I saw the Sea

Lillian Moore

Until I saw the sea
I did not know
that wind
could wrinkle water so.

I never knew
that sun
could splinter a whole sea of blue.

Nor
did I know before,
a sea breathes in and out
upon a shore.

Fishers of Men

(taken from John 21:1-14)

Karen Wilt / illustrated by Del Thompson

The Empty Net

Jesus had risen from the dead! The disciples had seen Him with their own eyes. Now He was gone, but He had told them to wait for Him.

Waiting was not easy. The days seemed long. The men had been fishermen before Christ had called them to be His disciples. They loved the sea and the roaring waves. But they had left everything to follow Christ.

They wanted to be busy again. One afternoon Peter had an idea. "I'm going fishing," he said to the others.

Several of the other disciples went with him. Quickly they gathered their net and left the village. They found a boat and pushed it into the sea.

Before long the men had sailed a short way from shore. They put weights on their net and let it slip into the water.

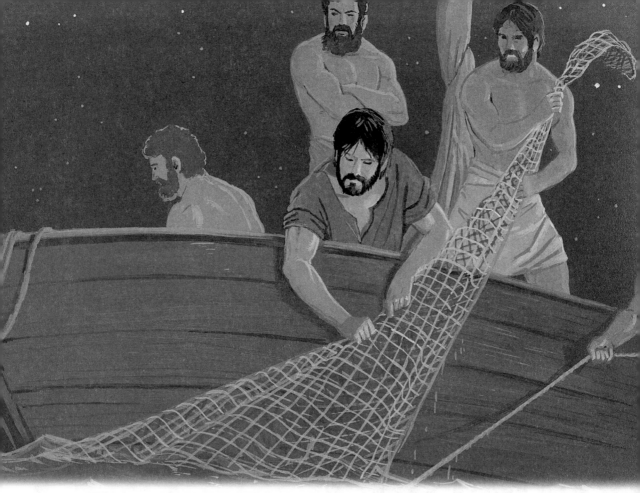

The waves rippled and rocked the boat.

"Have we caught anything?" Peter asked.

Thomas began pulling in the net. John pulled on the other end. Soon it lay in a heap on the deck. Not one fish wiggled in the tangled ropes. The net was empty.

They dropped it over the side again.

"It's getting dark," Nathanael said. "The fish should start swimming into our net now."

They waited and waited. Some of the men fell asleep. The stars twinkled, and the moon lit up the water.

At last they pulled in the net again. But it was as empty as before.

"I'm hungry," Thomas said.

"We can't eat until we catch some fish," Peter said. "Put the net back into the water."

The stars faded as the sun sent its first rays over the sea. The night had passed. The disciples pulled up the net. They were sure it would be full of great big fish this time.

Up came the net. All of the men helped to pull it in. It dripped large puddles of water onto the deck, but there were no fish.

The boat had drifted close to shore. The disciples saw a little fire. A man stood by it looking out at their boat.

"Have you any fish?" he called.

"No," they called back.

The man stepped closer to the water.

"Do you know who he is?" one of the disciples asked.

"No," the others answered.

"He must want some fish to eat this morning," Peter said.

The man on the shore called to them again. "Cast the net on the right side of the boat, and you will find fish."

They hauled the net to the other side.

"Careful or you will break it," Peter said.

"Maybe we should just go home. We have not caught anything all night. We won't catch anything now," Thomas said.

"Let's try one more time. We have the net over here already," Peter answered.

Quickly, they threw the net over the side and watched it sink beneath the waves.

"I think we have caught something," Peter said. "Pull it in."

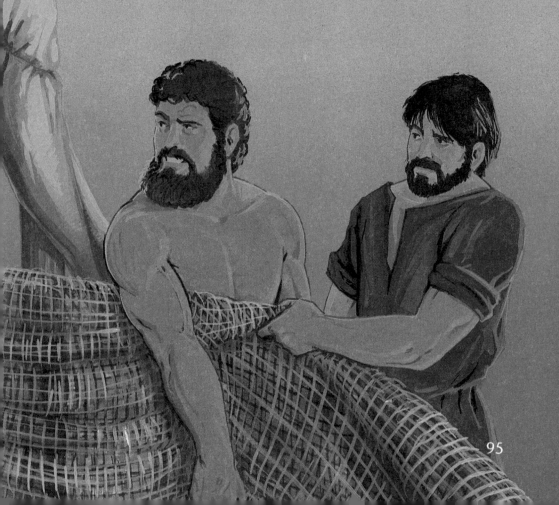

95

Follow Me

Two of the disciples tugged at the net. It wouldn't move. The others joined them. Slowly the net rose to the top. The scales of the fish in it glistened like silver treasure.

"Look!" James shouted.

"The net is too full," Nathanael said. "It is going to break."

"Can we get it into the boat?" another asked.

"No, we had better drag it to shore," Thomas said. The full net bumped against the side of the boat.

John shaded his eyes and peered at the shore. The man still stood there. The other disciples turned to John. "It is the Lord!" John said.

Before anyone else could speak, Peter grabbed
his fisherman's coat and jumped into the sea. He
swam quickly to shore. Finally his feet touched
the sandy bottom, and he ran up the beach.

The other disciples dragged the net along to
the shore. Then they too jumped over the side and
ran up the beach.

Jesus had a small fire with fish cooking on it for them. He had bread for them too.

"Bring the fish which you have now caught," He said to them.

Peter hurried to the boat and hauled in the net. He counted one hundred fifty-three fish in it. That was more than he had ever caught in one net!

"The net didn't break," he said to the others.

They shook their heads. They couldn't believe it had held so many.

Then Jesus called them to eat. He gave fish and bread to each of them.

The disciples ate the food quickly. They had been very hungry, and it tasted good.

After the men were done, Jesus spoke to them. They listened to every word He said. The disciples wanted to remember what He told them.

After the Lord had left them, the disciples put up their fishing net. They left the boat.

Soon the disciples were ready to go from town to town telling about the Lord Jesus.

They would not fish for fish anymore. Now they would fish only for men. The disciples would use the gospel to bring others to the Lord.

All of the disciples remembered the words Christ had said to them when He first called them. And at last they understood.

"Follow me, and I will make you fishers of men."
Matthew 4:19

Special Deeds

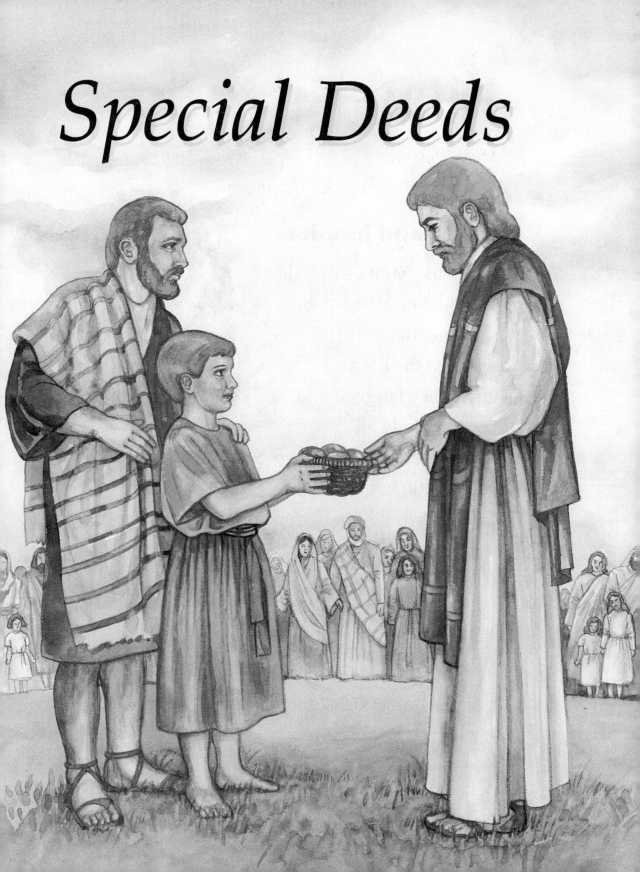

New Friends

Milly Howard /
illustrated by Del Thompson

Kristy and Juanita

It was Juanita's first day of school in America. She sat at her desk and watched the boys and girls. They laughed and talked quietly all around her. Juanita sighed. She could understand only a little English. She knew the American children would not understand her Spanish.

"Hi!" said a pretty girl with curly red hair.

Juanita knew that word. "Hi!" she said, smiling.

The girl began talking. Juanita shook her head. "I speak no English," she said.

The girl looked puzzled.

Just then Mr. Mullins called the class to order. They all stood to say the pledge to the American flag. Juanita stood up tall and proud with her hand over her heart. She could not say the pledge yet, but America was her new country. She was glad to go to school and planned to work hard to learn English.

The class said the pledges to the Christian flag and to the Bible. Then Mr. Mullins prayed. Juanita silently thanked God for her new Christian school.

Mr. Mullins spoke to the class in English. He called Juanita's name and held up some books and supplies for her. Juanita hurried to the front of the class to pick them up. As she carried them to her desk, the girl with the curly red hair smiled at her. Then the class began their work.

For a little while Juanita looked at the bright pictures in her schoolbooks. Then Mr. Mullins came to her desk. He handed Juanita a paper and said something to the redheaded girl. She pulled her chair up next to Juanita's.

"Juanita," Mr. Mullins said, "this is Kristy."

"Kristy?" Juanita asked, looking at the girl.

"Yes, my name is Kristy," the girl said. She showed Juanita the math work the class was doing. Soon Juanita was busy working too.

She quickly finished all the problems on her paper. "Done," she said.

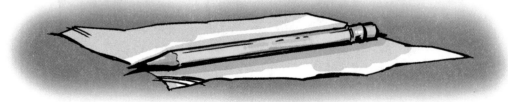

"Good!" Kristy exclaimed.

Juanita nodded. "Sí," she said.

Kristy and Juanita worked together the rest of the morning.

"It is time for lunch," Kristy said at last.

"Time? Lunch?" Juanita repeated.

"Sí!" Kristy pretended to eat a sandwich.

Juanita laughed. She understood that. She picked up her lunch box and followed Kristy.

The two girls washed their hands with soap and water at the sink and then went to the lunchroom.

That afternoon Mr. Mullins passed music books to the class. "Our school program is only two weeks away," he said. "We have learned many of the songs, but we have a lot of work to do."

Juanita liked to hear the class sing. She knew how to sing some of the songs in Spanish. Mr. Mullins let her sing one to the class.

"Would you like to sing Juanita's song in the program?" Mr. Mullins asked the class.

"Yes, sir!" was the answer.

Next they worked on Bible verses. Mr. Mullins wrote a verse for Juanita to learn.

He said the verse very slowly.

Juanita looked at the strange English words.

Mr. Mullins said it once again, a little at a time. Juanita repeated it, but she did not think she would ever remember all the words.

"I will help you," Kristy said.

Another Friend

Every day Kristy helped Juanita with her verse. Juanita's mother had explained the verse in Spanish, and Juanita said it in Spanish too.

One night Kristy went to dinner at Juanita's house. Juanita's mother made tacos. Juanita showed Kristy how to fill the cornmeal taco shell. She put in meat, beans, cheese, and tomatoes. Kristy ate two tacos.

Juanita ate her taco with hot sauce. Kristy tasted a little bit of the sauce, but she said it burned her mouth.

Juanita's mother made something special called *flan*. It tasted like sweet pudding covered with caramel. Kristy ate a piece.

After dinner Juanita tried to say her verse to Kristy. "Romans 5:8, 'But God commendeth his love toward us in that,—in that,—in that, . . .'" she stumbled.

" 'While we were yet sinners,' " Kristy said.

" 'While we were yet sinners,' " Juanita repeated.

" 'Christ died for us,' " said Kristy.

They finished just before Kristy's father came to take her home. "Good night, Juanita," Kristy said.

Juanita waved from the doorway. Maybe she would know her verse tomorrow.

On Saturday Juanita played in the park.

"Romans 5:8, 'But God commendeth his love toward us,' " she said as the swing went up. "Romans 5:8," she repeated as the swing came down.

A girl on the swing next to her listened to the words. "What are you saying?" she asked.

Juanita gulped. Did the girl want her to say the Bible verse? Maybe she did not know that Christ had died for her sins. Juanita tried hard to remember her verse. She must be able to say it.

" 'But God commendeth his love toward us in that, while we were yet sinners, Christ died for us,' " Juanita said. She had remembered every word!

"What does that mean?" the girl asked.

Juanita thought of all the English words she had learned. Could she explain to the girl that Christ would forgive her sins?

"Juanita!" a voice called.

Juanita turned around. "Kristy!" she said.

Kristy came up to the swings. "Tell Romans 5:8." Juanita said, pointing to the other girl.

"I'm Kristy. This is Juanita."

The other girl said, "I'm Sarah."

Juanita said, "Tell Sarah Romans 5:8."

Kristy said the verse. Then she said, "It means that God loves us and wants to forgive us for doing wrong." Juanita listened carefully. She wanted to know how to tell others about Jesus in English.

Kristy said, "If you want, you could come to a program at our school. We're going to say the verse and sing songs. Want to come?"

"I don't know. Maybe," the girl said. "Thank you for telling me about it."

Kristy nodded. "Okay." Then she said, "Want to go down the slide?"

The days passed quickly. Every day Kristy and Juanita prayed for the girl they had met in the park. Every day Juanita said her verse to Kristy.

The night of the program, Juanita's class marched out proudly. The time came to say the Bible verses. Juanita looked at the crowd. Sarah was sitting in the front row! She smiled at Juanita. Juanita almost waved at her.

"Romans 5:8 . . . ," Juanita began, and then she said the verse perfectly.

After the program Juanita found Kristy. Very carefully she said in English, "Thank you for helping me, Kristy. You are a kind friend."

"You are welcome," Kristy said. "De nada!"

Juanita laughed. "Let's go see Sarah," she said. "She is right over there."

Bread from Heaven *(a true story)*

Milly Howard / illustrated by Del Thompson

The Battlefield

Dwight Moody knelt beside the wounded soldier and felt his wrist. The man's lips moved, but his words did not carry above the rattle of the passing wagons. Moody leaned closer, barely making out the words.

"Pray for me, Mr. Moody," the man whispered.

"What's your name, Son?"

The answer was quiet. "Billy, sir."

"Before we pray, Billy, let me tell you something. God says that your soul can live forever with Him. He gave His own Son to die for your sins so that you can go to heaven.

" 'For God so loved the world that He gave His only begotten Son, that whosoever believeth in Him should not perish but have everlasting life.' Would you like to know Jesus as your Savior, Billy?"

"Yes, sir," Billy replied.

"Then let's pray," Mr. Moody said.

Billy trusted Jesus as his Savior. He lay back, smiling peacefully.

The general galloped past on his horse. He stopped and came back.

"Mr. Moody," the general said, "will you and your friends take charge of the wounded? Our men are already fighting down the road. We have no time to spare. We must join them."

"We are not doctors," said Mr. Moody. "But by God's grace we will do what we can."

"By God's grace it will have to be," the general said. He leaned over and shook Mr. Moody's hand. "We'll be back as soon as we can."

He galloped on with the soldiers.

The last wagons rumbled down the dirt road. The only sound on the battlefield was the moaning of the wounded soldiers.

Mr. Moody called his friends together. "We came to give the gospel to these soldiers," he said. "But now God asks us to do more. I know we are not doctors, but we can be of some help.

"Only God knows when the army can return. Do what you can for the wounded and pray with them."

A man nearby pushed himself up on one elbow. He called "Water! Please, water!"

"There's a stream a short walk away," Mr. Moody told his friends. "Take as many canteens as you can carry. I will do what I can until you return."

The young men gathered up the canteens and ran to the stream. Mr. Moody rolled up his sleeves and began to work. He wrapped wounds with clean cloth and prayed with each soldier.

The Prayer Meeting

Soon Mr. Moody's friends returned with full canteens. Quickly they moved among the soldiers, giving them water. As they helped the thirsty soldiers drink, they told them about God's love for them. Many soldiers trusted Christ as their Savior that long afternoon.

The sun began to set behind the hills. Mr. Moody and the other men helping gathered to talk.

"What about food?" asked one.

"Yes, it has been hours since the soldiers have eaten," replied another.

"Let's see what we can find in the knapsacks," Mr. Moody said. "Perhaps the soldiers carried enough rations to feed at least this many."

The men emptied the knapsacks and piled the rations on a sheet of canvas in front of Mr. Moody. He shook his head slowly. "There is not enough food for everyone," he said. "The weak and wounded must have food soon or they will die."

The men looked at each other. The nearest town was miles away.

"I guess I could walk to the town," suggested one of the men.

"No," Mr. Moody said, "every man is needed here."

Mr. Moody knelt on the ground beside the sheet of canvas. The other men knelt beside him and began to pray. They asked God to send bread, but they had no idea how their prayer would be answered.

After they had prayed, Mr. Moody stood up. "Now, let's leave the problem of food with God," he said.

The men went back to work. All through the night, they cared for the soldiers. Tired and still hungry, they welcomed the first light of dawn. Then in the stillness they heard the sound of a wagon.

"Is the army coming back?" someone asked.

They all peered through the morning mist. A large wagon rumbled up the road and stopped in front of them. It was filled to the top with loaves of bread!

The driver jumped down from the wagon seat. "Who's in charge here?" he asked.

"I am," replied Mr. Moody. He held out his hand. "I'm Dwight Moody."

The driver shook his hand. "Glad to meet you, Dr. Moody. My name is Stevens."

Mr. Moody smiled. "We're not doctors, sir, only men who wanted to help the soldiers."

"I want to help too," said the driver. "I saw the army go past last night. When I went to bed, I couldn't sleep. All I could think about was the wounded soldiers left behind. I woke my wife and told her that we must take food to the wounded soldiers. We had only a little bread in the house.

"While my wife was busy baking more, I hitched up the wagon. I drove from Martin Street all the way to the church on South Avenue, waking up my neighbors. They gave me all the bread in their houses.

"At last my wagon was full. When I got home, my wife's bread was done. I piled her bread on top. I drove away feeling as though the Lord Himself was sending me."

Tears came to Mr. Moody's eyes. "Mr. Stevens, the Lord did send you. Let us give thanks for His faithfulness."

All bowed their heads as Mr. Moody prayed, thanking the Lord for the bread. When he finished, he clapped Mr. Stevens on the shoulder and said, "Now let's unload the bread from heaven and feed the soldiers."

The Farmer and the Donkey

Karen Wilt / illustrated by Tim Davis

Cast

Narrator
Farmer
Son
Glum, the donkey
Baker
Blacksmith

Tailor
Tailor's wife
Miller
Townsfolk
Storekeeper

Off to Town

Narrator: Once upon a time there lived an old farmer, his son, and their gray-eared donkey named Glum. Now the old farmer worked hard on his farm, and his son almost always helped him. The old farmer had only one problem. He always tried to take everyone's advice. Then, one day . . .

Farmer: Time for us to leave, Son. Hi-ho! We must hurry along to town to sell the donkey.

Son: Coming, Father. I'll fetch Glum's rope.

Glum: Hee-haw. Hee-haw.

Narrator: Soon the old farmer had bolted the door and had set off down the dirt road with his son and Glum, the donkey. Whom should they meet but their friend the baker, pushing his cart of rolls and sweet cakes.

Baker: Hello there! What's this? A fine donkey trotting merrily along, and you two scurrying along to keep up. One of you should ride him.

Farmer: That is good advice, friend baker. Climb up, Son, and we'll be on our way to town to sell our donkey.

Baker: Such a fine donkey should bring a good price—especially with those long gray ears he has.

Glum: Hee-haw. Hee-haw.

Narrator: So the two set off for the town again with Glum, the donkey, carrying the farmer's son, who bobbed up and down with each step. The farmer marched along in front of them.

Son: Father, here comes the blacksmith. He must be on his way home from town.

Blacksmith: Good morning, friend farmer. What's this? Your son rides while you walk? People will surely think he is lazy.

Farmer: You are right. Jump down, Son. Let me ride.

Blacksmith: Yes, let your son's strong legs trot along while you rest your tired bones.

Farmer: Thank you, kind blacksmith. My friends always have such helpful advice. Now we must be off to town to sell this donkey.

Blacksmith: Glad I could help. You have a fine-looking donkey. What beautiful, long, gray ears he has!

Glum: Hee-haw. Hee-haw.

You Cannot Please Everyone

Narrator: An hour later the farmer and his son reached the town. They trotted by the tailor's house as the tailor and his wife sat on their porch.

Tailor's Wife: Tut, tut, and look at that; the farmer rides along while his little boy has to run as best he can to keep up. For shame!

Farmer: Well, well. What can I do?

Tailor: Why, your fine donkey could surely carry both of you!

Farmer: Oh, what good advice. I should have thought of it myself. Thank you, kind tailor.

Son: Should I climb up behind you, Father?

Farmer: Yes, come along. With both of us riding, we will reach the marketplace in no time at all.

Narrator: The farmer and his son again set off, bouncing up and down and back and forth as Glum wobbled down the street. Before long the miller met them with his sack of wheat slung over his arm.

Miller: What's this? Such a sad donkey. I would never wish to carry such a heavy load as he has been carrying. He looks like he might fall over and die. His long gray ears are drooping so low they almost reach the ground.

Farmer: Well, I guess this is a heavy load for Glum.

Miller: Indeed! You should carry him!

Farmer: We will. Son, find a long pole. We can tie Glum to it with his rope and carry him between us.

Son: Yes, sir. Here's one by the street.

Miller: Your donkey's long gray ears have perked up already.

Farmer: Good. We are taking him to the marketplace to sell him. No one will pay for him if he is worn out from carrying us. Thank you for the good advice.

Miller: You're welcome! Take care of your donkey.

Narrator: At last the two set off again with Glum's feet tied to a pole. The farmer carried one end of the pole, and his son carried the other end. They shuffled along slowly till they reached the cobblestone streets of the marketplace.

Townsfolk: Look, look! What's this?

Storekeeper: A man and a boy are carrying a donkey!

Townsfolk: What a strange sight!

Storekeeper: I can't believe anyone would do something so foolish.

Townsfolk: Oh, ho-ho-ho-ho-ha-ha-ha-ha! How foolish! How silly!

Glum: Hee-haw. Hee-haw.

Farmer: Hush, hush! You're frightening my donkey.

Glum: Hee-Haw! HEE-HAW! HEE-HAW!

Narrator: At that Glum pulled and kicked till his rope broke and the pole snapped in two. He rolled over and began to run.

Glum: HEE-HAW! HEE-HAW!

Farmer: Quick! Catch him!

Son *(panting)*: Stop him! He's running away!

Townsfolk: There he goes! All you can see are his long gray ears.

Farmer: Alas, my donkey is gone. I foolishly took bad advice.

Son: Now we cannot ride, carry, or even sell Glum.

Farmer: I have learned my lesson too late. In trying to please everyone, I have pleased no one.

Have You Seen My Dog?

Milly Howard / illustrated by Timothy Banks

Where Is Lady?

Pete jumped down the porch steps. He pushed open the gate to the back yard.

"Here, Lady!" he called. There was no answering bark. The fenced yard was empty. He frowned. "That dog is gone again," Pete said. He got his bike out of the shed and pushed it to the front yard. He stopped beside his father.

"Dad, have you seen Lady?" he asked.

"Why no," said his father. "Is she gone again?"

"Yes, sir," Pete said. "May I go look for her?"

His father said, "Why don't you ask Allen to help you?" Pete rode down the street. Allen was outside mowing the lawn.

"Have you seen Lady?" Pete asked.

132

Allen stopped the mower. "No, not this morning. Is she gone again?" he asked.

Pete nodded. "She has been wandering off since her puppies died. She must be looking for them."

Allen said, "Could you finish this last bit? I'll go ask Mom." Pete took over and then put the mower away.

"My mother said it's okay," Allen said. He rolled his bike out of the shed. "Let's go!"

The two boys pedaled up the street. They didn't see Lady anywhere.

As they turned the corner of Maple Lane and Main Street, their friend Henry waved at them from his yard.

"Hello, Henry!" called Pete.

"What are you two doing?" Henry asked.

"We're looking for my dog," Pete said. "She got out again, and we can't find her anywhere."

"Lady? She ran past here early this morning," said Henry.

"Which way did she go?" Allen asked.

"Out that way." Henry pointed toward the lumberyard.

"Thanks, Henry." The two boys pedaled away.

"Here, Lady!" Pete whistled for her as they rode past the lumberyard.

Allen braked suddenly. "There she is!"

"Lady!" Pete yelled. "Come here!"

The boys turned into the lumberyard. They rode in and out of the stacks of lumber. They could not see Lady. They called and whistled, but there was no answer.

A tall man stopped them as they turned a corner. "What are you kids doing? You can't ride through here. This isn't a playground."

"We're sorry, sir," said Pete. "We were just looking for my dog."

The man put his hands on his hips and frowned. "A dog?"

"Yes, sir," said Allen. "I thought I saw her go around that corner."

"A big dog?" The man held his hands about knee high. "Red, floppy ears, big brown eyes?"

"That's Lady!" said Allen.

"She went through a broken board in the back fence," the man replied. "There's a vacant lot over there."

"Thank you!" called the boys as they rode away. They pedaled down the side road to the vacant lot.

"Look," said Allen. He pointed to an old shed almost hidden in the weeds.

A muffled bark came from the shed.

"Lady!" cried Pete. He got off his bike and ran the rest of the way to the shed door.

Lady looked up at the boys and wagged her tail. Then she nudged the squirming, furry bodies beside her.

"Puppies! Lady has puppies!" said Allen.

Pete dropped to his knees beside Lady. "Allen, these aren't puppies!"

Lady's New Family

"What are they?" Allen asked. He bent over. "You must be kidding!" He laughed. "Kittens!"

"Remember when Lady's puppies died?" Pete said. "She wandered around the neighborhood for days looking for them. I guess she must have found the kittens alone and adopted them."

"Something must have happened to their mother," said Allen. "I wonder how this will work out."

"So do I," Pete said.

Pete stroked Lady's head. "Well," he said at last, "we can take the kittens home in our bike baskets. Lady will follow us."

Lady whimpered as the boys put the kittens into the wire baskets. Then she ran alongside the bikes all the way home.

"Mom, Dad!" Pete shouted as they turned into the driveway. "Come and see what we have!"

His mother and father came to the kitchen door. Pete and Allen put the kittens on the grass.

"How pretty," said Mrs. Wei, picking up one of the kittens. "Where did you find them?"

"We didn't find them. Lady did," said Allen.

"Lady found them?" Mr. Wei raised his eyebrows.

"Yes, sir. They were in an old shed near the lumberyard," said Allen.

"Where was their mother?" asked Mrs. Wei.

"We don't know," Pete replied. "Lady was taking care of them."

"You mean she adopted them?" asked Mr. Wei.

"Yes, sir," said Allen.

"I've heard of animals adopting other animals before," said Mr. Wei. "But it doesn't happen often."

Allen stood up suddenly. "Hey, Pete, why don't you telephone the newspaper office? This would make a good story."

Mrs. Wei carried the kittens inside. Pete and Allen raced for the telephone.

By the time the newspaper reporter arrived, the kittens were well used to their new home. The reporter took a picture of Lady licking her kittens.

A few days later, Pete proudly showed the newspaper to his classmates.

Almost every day after that, someone would knock at the kitchen door wanting to see Lady and her kittens. Pete enjoyed taking his friends to meet Lady. The kittens grew bigger and bigger.

One day as Pete made a peanut butter sandwich at the kitchen counter, one little black kitten stalked him from behind and made a flying leap.

"Peanut butter pawprints? On my kitchen counter?" asked his mother. She handed him a cloth.

There was a ripping sound behind them.

"My curtains!" she cried.

Mr. Wei took the kitten off the curtains. "I think it's time the kittens learned about the big outdoors," he said firmly.

Pete and his father took Lady and her kittens into the back yard. All went well for a few days. Then the neighborhood dogs discovered the kittens. The noise was awful! Even Pete put his hands over his ears.

"Sorry, Son," Pete's father said. "They've got to go. You know we will find good homes for them."

Pete was not surprised to find the kittens gone when he came home from school the next day. He ran to the back yard. Lady lay in the grass, her head on her paws. She didn't look up.

Pete stopped beside his father. "Dad, Lady sure looks lonely."

"Just watch," said Mr. Wei. There was a slight movement on the doghouse roof. A small black bundle of fur stretched and arched its back lazily. The kitten looked at the gloomy dog below. It switched its tail back and forth. Then it sprang!

"Woof!" barked the surprised dog.

Away dashed the kitten with Lady happily chasing it.

"We left one for Lady," said Mr. Wei. "I think she will have her paws full!"

The Little Maid

Karen Wilt/
illustrated by Keith Neely   *(taken from II Kings 5)*

Captain Naaman, the Leper

One day enemy soldiers came from a faraway country. They came like robbers and took away many of God's people to be slaves. One little Hebrew girl was taken to Captain Naaman's house. There she served as a maid to Captain Naaman's wife. The lady was kind, but the little maid missed her home and her family very much.

Now Captain Naaman was sick. He had a dreadful illness called leprosy. Large sores that would not heal had spread over his skin. All the doctors in Syria did not know how to make him well.

One afternoon the little maid was busy helping her mistress, but her mistress did not say a word. Later, the little maid found her crying in the garden.

"Oh, Mistress, do not weep," she said, bringing her a cool cloth to wipe away her tears.

Her mistress shook her head. "Captain Naaman is very ill," she said.

Tears came to the little maid's eyes. "Will he get better?" she asked.

"No," her mistress answered, "Captain Naaman will never fight in great battles again. He will never get better."

"I wish I could help him," the little maid said. "If only my master would go to the prophet Elisha in my home country, Elisha could heal him."

Just then a servant walked past the garden and heard them talking.

"What did you say, child?" he asked.

"I heard of many great works that Elisha did when I lived near him. He is a prophet of the one true God," she said.

The servant hurried on his way, but he did not forget the girl's words.

"Master," he said, kneeling beside Naaman. "May we take you to Elisha? Your wife's little maid says that he can heal you. You can be well again!"

"Elisha?" Naaman asked.

"Yes, he is a prophet of God. The little maid is sure he can heal you," the servant said.

"Then we will leave tomorrow," said Naaman.

Naaman's servants packed silver, gold, and beautiful garments to pay Elisha. Then Naaman climbed into the chariot.

Days passed as they traveled on the hot, dusty roads. The horses trotted mile after mile, carrying Captain Naaman to Elisha. As his chariot bumped along, Naaman thought about the prophet of God. Would Elisha stand in front of Naaman and call loudly to God to heal him? Would he strike the sores with his hand? Would the sores just disappear? Could the little maid's God heal him?

At last Captain Naaman arrived in Elisha's city. His chariot came to a stop in front of Elisha's door.

Captain Naaman stepped down from the chariot.

Inside the house Elisha spoke quietly to his servant. The servant hurried to the door. He opened the door before Naaman could knock.

"Naaman," the servant said, "Elisha sent me to tell you to go and wash in the Jordan River seven times, and your skin will be clean. You will be made well."

"Wash in the Jordan seven times?" Naaman said in an angry voice.

Naaman turned to his servants. "I thought Elisha would at least come out to talk to me. He just sent his servant to tell me to wash in the dirty Jordan River. I can go to the clean rivers at home to wash!" He stomped away, muttering to himself. Into his chariot he climbed.

"Master," one servant said, "will you go to the Jordan River?"

Captain Naaman frowned. "No! Take me home!" he ordered.

Naaman's servants turned sadly back to the chariots. Their master would never be made well. The servant turned again to Captain Naaman.

"Master," he said, "if Elisha had asked you to do something hard, would you have done it?"

Another servant joined the first. "Yes, Master, if Elisha had asked you to do a great thing, you would have done it. Can't you do this easy thing?"

"We want you to be made well, Master," the servants said.

Naaman looked at his faithful servants. "Yes," he said. "You're right. Take me to the Jordan River."

In the Jordan River

Naaman watched the trees by the roadside and thought about Elisha. Could Elisha and the little maid's God heal him? If He could, then He would be greater than all the doctors Captain Naaman had seen. They had not been able to heal him. If the little maid's God could heal him, then Naaman would know that He was the one true and living God.

At last they could see the Jordan River. As the chariot stopped, Naaman saw the muddy water lap the riverbank. He did not want to go into the muddy water. But his servants were waiting to help him from the chariot, and he had to keep his word.

The servants stood on the bank. Captain Naaman stepped into the river. The water was warm, but it was so muddy he could not see his toes as they squished in the mud. He waded in until the water reached his waist.

Each servant held his breath. Would Naaman's leprosy be gone?

Naaman dunked under the water. The servants looked closely at him. The leprosy was still there.

Down Naaman dunked again. But the sores did not even begin to heal.

Again the third time he dunked himself. Four, five, six times the muddy water closed above his head. One more time would be seven.

Captain Naaman dipped his hands and arms under the water; then he dunked his head under. The servants leaned out over the river to watch Naaman come up.

Slowly, slowly Naaman stood up. He shook the muddy water out of his eyes and looked at his hands and arms.

"Has the little maid's God healed you?" the servants called.

"Yes!" Captain Naaman shouted. "I am well! My skin is as clean as can be!"

The servants almost tripped over each other as they joyfully helped Captain Naaman out of the water.

Every sore was gone. Captain Naaman could never again be called a leper. Quickly, Naaman rode back to find Elisha.

"Now I know your God is the true and living God," Naaman said to Elisha. "He is the only God. I will trust in Him."

Naaman called his servants. They held up the riches Naaman had brought. "Take these, Elisha, in payment," Naaman said.

Elisha shook his head. "No, God made you well, Naaman. I cannot take these things."

Naaman turned to leave. "I will always worship the true God. Thank you, Elisha."

Days later Naaman arrived at home. "Captain Naaman is home!" the servants shouted.

The little maid ran outside with her mistress.

Captain Naaman stepped down from the chariot. He showed them his clean skin, glowing with health.

"The little maid's God healed me of my leprosy," he said. "He is the only true God."

Annie Sullivan (a true story)

Becky Davis and Eileen M. Berry

illustrated by Stephanie True and Johanna Berg

Tewksbury

"What is this place?" Ten-year-old Annie Sullivan clutched her brother Jimmie's arm and squinted at the building in front of her. With her other hand she rubbed her red, puffy eyes. She hoped the man who had brought them here would not think she had been crying. Her eyes were swollen because of a sickness that had left her almost blind.

"This is Tewksbury," answered the man. "A home for the poor. You and your brother will be living here for a while."

Annie did not think much of Tewksbury. Many of the people there were old or sick. Like Annie and Jimmie, they all had no one to care for them. Annie stayed close to Jimmie. "I'll take care of you," she told him. He was lame, and the pain in his legs grew worse every day.

One morning Annie woke up and found that Jimmie's cot was gone. He had died in the night.

Annie spent days sitting still and staring into the empty space by her bed. She did not want to play or even to talk.

One day a girl about Annie's age walked over. "Would you like me to read to you?" she asked. Annie listened as her new friend read stories from books. She tried to see the pictures in the books, but she saw only colored shapes. "I want to learn to read too," she thought.

Annie told her wishes to Miss Maggie, a lady in charge of Tewksbury. Maggie thought for a moment. "I have heard of a school where they teach blind people to read. It's called Perkins. I have even read of a lady at Perkins who is both blind and deaf. Laura Bridgman is her name.  She has learned many things at the school." Her voice became sad. "But it costs money to go there. You don't have any money, Annie. You may as well face it. You will be at Tewksbury for the rest of your life."

"No, I won't," said Annie. "Somehow, I'm going to go to that school and learn to read."

The thought of school never left Annie's mind. One day some men came to inspect Tewksbury.

"This is your chance, Annie," whispered a friend. "One of those men is Mr. Sanborn. He knows about Perkins—that school for the blind."

Annie ran up to the men as they were about to leave. "Mr. Sanborn!" she cried. "I want to learn to read! Please let me go to Perkins."

Annie was told to go back to her room. But she kept waiting and hoping. Several weeks went by. Then Miss Maggie sent for her.

"Annie, I have wonderful news! This letter says that you can go to Perkins School for the Blind . . . and you won't have to pay a cent!"

Perkins

September came, and Annie rode a train to Perkins School. She was almost fifteen years old, but the teachers put her in the first grade.

The first graders at the school for the blind couldn't see Annie, but they knew she was much older than they were.

"Big Annie! Big Annie!" they teased.

Annie gritted her teeth. "I'll put up with anything as long as I can learn to read," she said.

Because Annie's eyes were bad, she learned to read raised letters by feeling their shapes. She would sit for hours without even changing positions. She read stories of princes and giants, stories of great leaders in history, and stories of Bible heroes. "There's a whole new world inside books," she thought. "What would it be like to see the pictures?"

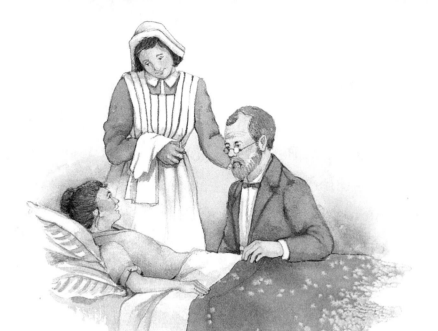

Not long before Annie finished school, a doctor tried an operation on her eyes. The doctor removed the strips of cloth from her eyes afterwards. Annie held her breath. "Annie," the doctor asked, "can you see me?"

Annie opened her eyes.

The doctor's face seemed to swim in the air. Then slowly, slowly it became clear.

"I can see you!" she whispered. She looked around the room. "I can see the nurse and the bed and the window. Not just shapes—the real things!" Annie gripped the sheet tightly. "It's better than any picture in a book."

Annie finished school in just six years. She began to think about what she should do next.

"I have a letter you might like to see," a friend at Perkins said to Annie one day. "The Keller family in Alabama has a six-year-old daughter, Helen, who can't see or hear. She needs a good teacher. Are you interested in the job?"

Annie frowned. A girl who couldn't see or hear! How could she possibly teach a child like that? But then she thought of Miss Bridgman, the blind and deaf lady at Perkins who had become her friend. People could "talk" to Miss Bridgman by spelling words into her hand with their fingers. Could Helen be taught in the same way? Annie made her decision. "It will be a big job," she said, "but I'm willing to try."

Annie didn't have much to pack. In a few days she was on the train to Tuscumbia, Alabama. She stared out the window, thinking of the little girl who couldn't see or hear. The clack-a-clack, clack-a-clack of the wheels rattled beneath her. "Blind and deaf, blind and deaf," they seemed to say.

"But I was blind too." Annie sat up straighter. "I learned to read. And I know the finger alphabet. I'm sure I can help Helen Keller to understand me. I'll do my best."

When Annie got to the Keller home, the first thing she saw was a little girl with messy hair and a dirty dress. "So this is Helen," she thought. Annie gave Helen the doll she had brought for her.

Tuscumbia

At supper Helen sat beside Annie. Annie watched as Helen's mother tried to get her to eat. Helen just threw her spoon and grabbed food off her mother's plate. Then she ran away from the table.

Annie went to find Helen. She laid the doll in Helen's arms. Then she spelled the word *d-o-l-l* into Helen's hand. Helen smiled.

But when Annie tried to put the doll away, Helen became angry. She kicked Annie and hit her with her fists. "Before I can teach Helen," said Annie, "she must learn to obey."

Helen had never learned to obey. Her family felt sorry for her, and they had always let her do as she liked. Now Annie had an idea. "I must take Helen away from here," she said.

Helen's father let Annie take Helen to a little house nearby.

At first Annie had a hard time. Helen fought when Annie tried to dress her or put her to bed. Sometimes Annie wanted to become angry too. Sometimes she sat down and cried. But she kept trying. And she never let Helen get her own way.

Slowly, Helen began to change. She stopped hitting and kicking. She went to bed without fights. She learned to be quiet when she did not get what she wanted. One day she even let Annie hold her on her lap.

"It's time we moved back to the big house," Annie told Helen's mother and father. "I think I can teach Helen, now that she knows she must obey."

Soon Helen learned how to repeat Annie's
hand spellings with her fingers. But Annie could
tell that Helen didn't understand. She didn't
know that *d-o-l-l* meant the soft plaything that she
held in her arms, or that *c-a-k-e*
meant the food that tasted
good. Every lesson was
like a game to Helen.
Annie often lay awake at
night, thinking. "How
will I ever make her
understand?"

Several months passed. One warm day, Annie and Helen went outside to the water pump for a drink. Helen pushed her arms under the water. Annie, just as she always did, spelled the word into Helen's hand. "*W-a-t-e-r, w-a-t-e-r,*" she spelled as the cool liquid gushed over Helen's hands and arms.

Suddenly, Helen stood straight up. She was smiling. Her fingers quickly spelled the word back into Annie's hand. She spelled the word again and again. Something was different.

"She understands," Annie whispered. Then she looked up at the sky. "She understands!" she shouted. She laughed and threw her arms around Helen. "Oh, Helen, now you understand what words are. Now I can teach you to talk with your fingers just as well as anybody else can talk with his mouth."

Helen pointed to the pump. "*P-u-m-p,*" Annie spelled into her hand. Helen ran to a tree and pointed. "*T-r-e-e,*" Annie spelled. Then Helen reached out and touched Annie. "*T-e-a-c-h-e-r.*" Helen learned hundreds of new words that day.

At last, Annie Sullivan had freed Helen Keller from her dark, silent prison.

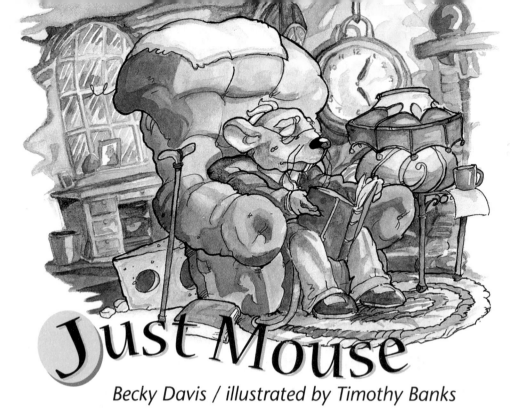

Just Mouse

Becky Davis / illustrated by Timothy Banks

A Noise at the Door

In the back of an old brown house in a tiny hole under a rotten board there lived a mouse. He was an old gray mouse with trembly whiskers and a long gray tail. He lived alone and talked to no one but himself. Sometimes he muttered, "I like the quiet. I like living alone. I don't want to help anybody. I don't want anybody helping me. I never want to see anybody else." And so he lived, waking up alone and going to bed alone, never seeing anyone.

One day Mouse lay curled up in his chair, reading. The thunder crashed, the wind howled, and the rain battered against the window. "It's good to have a book to read on such a stormy afternoon," he muttered. "And it's very good to be alone."

He had not been reading long when a scurrying, mouselike sound startled him. "I never hear noises like that unless I make them," he said. "I wonder what it could be."

Taking his old brown cane, he left his hole and peered around the empty house. There, not far from his doorway, he saw a wet little mouse lying very still.

"Humph. He must have fainted." Mouse turned to go back into his hole. "I don't want to help anybody, and I don't want anybody helping me." He stopped. The mouse was very little, and he looked so weak and hungry.

"I guess I could just help him dry off." Mouse shrugged. "And maybe I could give him some cheese."

After only a few moments in the dry, warm hole, the little mouse woke up enough to eat some cheese. "Oh, thank you, sir," he said. "You're a kind mouse. What is your name?"

"Just Mouse," answered Mouse. "Nobody has ever called me anything but Mouse."

"I'm Preston," said the small mouse. "I came looking for help for my two brothers. They're caught in a mousetrap. Will you come and help me rescue them?"

Mouse's whiskers trembled. "I don't want to help anybody. . . ." He stopped when he saw a big tear roll down Preston's face.

"Just this once," Mouse said slowly. "And then you really must go away and leave me alone."

"Oh, thank you! Thank you!" Preston scampered around the room. Mouse picked up his old brown cane and followed Preston out of the house and down the trail. "At least the storm has stopped," he muttered.

"They're in a house over that hill," Preston said as he pointed.

"Huh," grunted Mouse. He didn't like this idea of helping. He only liked being alone.

"There they are!" Preston said. "Hold on! We're going to save you!" he called.

Mouse looked through the cellar window to see two frightened little mice comforting each other in the corner of a cage.

Mouse to the Rescue

Mouse thought about the problem for a moment.

"Maybe I can do something with my cane." Mouse led the way into the room through a crack in the wall. Being careful not to get too close to the trap, he wedged his cane under the cage. Together Mouse and Preston pried up the cage. Two little mice scrambled out.

"Oh, thank you! Thank you for saving us!" They scampered around and around, squeaking joyfully. "Who are you?"

"I'm Mouse," said Mouse. "Just Mouse."

"I'm Patton," said one mouse.

"I'm Porter," said the other.

Mouse grunted. "You three get along home now and stay out of trouble!" He turned to leave. But Preston, Patton, and Porter scampered down the road beside him. Before Mouse could say anything else to them, Patton squealed, "Look!"

There against a wall a big black cat had cornered two little frightened mice. "We must rescue them!" cried Porter. "But how?"

"I don't want to help. . .," Mouse began. But he thought about the big black cat eating up the two wee, little mice. He shuddered. Then his mind worked quickly.

"You three little ones run to make the cat chase you over here," he said. "Then I'll fix him."

As brave as tigers, Preston, Patton, and Porter ran toward the black cat. "Catch us if you can!" they yelled, and made faces at him.

174

The black cat yowled and spat. He forgot the two mice he had cornered and jumped toward the three mice brothers.

Quick as a flash, Preston, Patton, and Porter raced toward Mouse. He stood right in the way of the big black cat.

"Take that!" he cried, and poked the cat sharply in the nose three times.

"MeOWWWW!" yowled the cat, and he ran away as fast as he could go. The two little mice were safe.

"Thank you, thank you!" they cried. "We were sure we would never live to see another mouse! Who are you, sir?"

"I'm just Mouse," said Mouse. "Nothing but Mouse."

"I'm William," said one mouse.

"I'm George," said the other. "We'll go home with you."

"Oh, no," said Mouse. "I like the quiet. I like living alone. I don't want to help anybody, and I don't want anybody helping me."

But when he turned to go to his house, Preston, Patton, Porter, William, and George trailed right along behind him.

"Go away!"

They still followed him.

Finally Mouse gave up and said nothing more.

When he got home, Preston, Patton, Porter, William, and George gathered around him. "We don't think Mouse is a good enough name for you," said George. "We've decided to call you Granddaddy Mouse."

For the first time in all his life, Mouse's little nose twitched as he smiled a wee little smile. "I don't think that's such a bad name." He sat down in his big easy chair.

"Maybe—" Mouse said as Preston climbed into his lap . . .

"Maybe—" he smiled as Patton, William, and Porter skipped happily about . . .

"Just maybe," he sighed as George hugged him, "helping might be worth something after all."

The Wright Flyer

Nellie Ashe Cooper

For hundreds of years people believed that man could learn to fly like birds.

In the late 1800s, a German named Otto Lilienthal flew gliders with wings of different shapes.

He died in a crash before he could test all he had learned. In Dayton, Ohio, two brothers heard about his death and began to wonder if flight was possible. Orville and Wilbur Wright read everything they could find about flying.

The brothers made a glider that was guided with strings like a kite. They went to the coast of North Carolina and tested it more than a thousand times. They studied engines until they could build one that was powerful but not too heavy for their flying machine.

Clouds hung low, and winds howled across a high hill at Kitty Hawk, North Carolina, on December 17, 1903. The Wright brothers and their helpers lifted the machine onto the starting track. Orville lay along the bottom wing to guide it. Down the track it rolled and lifted off. It flew for 120 feet before it skidded to a stop in the sand. For the first time a pilot had flown a powered flying machine—an airplane!

Orville and Wilbur did not become famous right away. Many people did not believe that they had really flown. In 1908 they started making public flights, and their *Wright Flyer* became known around the world.

Test Flights

Make a paper airplane.

Start with a sheet of 8½"x11" paper.
Fold it in half the long way.
Run your thumbnail along the fold to crease it.

Open the paper and **fold** down the two
top corners to the center.

Fold the sides down again to the center.

Turn the paper over.
Fold the plane in half along the center fold.
Fold the right wing down, beginning at the
nose of the plane. **Turn** the plane over and
fold the left wing down, beginning at the
nose of the plane.

Open out the wings and tape them together.
The wings should slant slightly up.

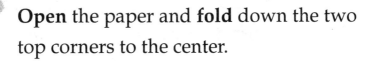

The Pineyridge Snowstorm

(a Paul Bunyan tall tale)

Milly Howard / illustrated by Jim Harris and Timothy Banks

Snowstorm!

At the first flurry of snow, the lumberjacks dropped their axes and scrambled up the nearest trees. Snow quickly piled up beneath them as the flurry turned into the first snowstorm of the year. Many, many feet of snow covered the ground in an hour. The lumberjacks climbed higher into the treetops as their camp disappeared under the snow.

Johnny Inkslinger clung to his icy branch. He wished that he had not stepped outside the door for a breath of air.

"Brr!" The little bookkeeper shivered. "If only Paul Bunyan were here," he said to himself. "He would rescue us!"

Far above him, Johnny saw a big hole. Shaking with cold, he climbed up. Soon he was curled up in the hollow tree, fast asleep.

Johnny didn't know it, but Paul Bunyan wasn't far away. Paul had been away visiting his other logging camps. The camps were strung across the north from Maine to Minnesota. But now he was on his way back to Pineyridge. He walked along slowly, taking only mile-long steps.

Suddenly, Paul shivered and pulled up the collar of his wool shirt.

Babe, the famous blue ox, saw the snow first. She tossed her enormous horns and began to trot.

"Whoa, Babe!" called Paul. "People will think there's an earthquake!"

The lumberjacks waved their hats and cheered when they saw Paul.

"I guess it's a good thing that wasn't a big snowstorm." Paul chuckled as he took the men out of the trees. "Even the trees would have been covered then!"

As he looked around, Paul saw a wisp of blue smoke coming from a snowdrift. He tunneled down to the cook house and wiped off a window. When he peered inside, the busy cooks hardly looked up.

"Weren't you scared?" Paul opened the door and called to Flapjack Freddy.

"Scared? Of what?" The cook looked up for a moment.

"Why, scared of the snowstorm," Paul said.

"Too busy!" The chief cook went back to work. "Too busy to look outside!"

"Watch out there," Flapjack called. One of the boys almost skated off the edge of the giant griddle. It smoked and hissed as the boys skated around with big slabs of bacon strapped to their feet.

"Ready with the batter for Paul Bunyan's pancakes!" Flapjack waved to the other cooks. They rolled the huge barrel of pancake batter over to the griddle. Other cooks stood ready with snow shovels to turn the pancakes as the batter was piped onto the hot griddle.

"You were too busy to see the snow!" Paul watched the cooks pour the batter on the griddle. "Now I had better get busy myself."

Paul climbed back to the top of the snowdrift. "Get some snowshoes and some more axes, men. We have ten thousand trees to deliver!"

Paul harnessed Babe and dug out some big logging chains. He looped one end of the chain around a treetop and the other to Babe's harness.

"Pull, Babe."

Babe tossed her horns and pulled. The tree flew out of the snow like a rabbit out of his hole!

The Hollow Tree

The men went to work chopping off the tree branches. Paul and Babe moved on to another treetop. Soon ten thousand logs were piled on the hill beside Pineyridge River.

"The ice is too thick," said Paul's foreman. "The logs won't break it. How will we get them downriver?"

Paul grinned and called for Babe. She pawed the snow as he unhitched the chains. Then with a huge leap, the blue ox slid down the hill. Babe hit the ice so hard that it broke into tiny pieces and fell as hail all the way to Boston!

Paul gave the logs a push, and they rolled into
the water with a mighty splash. Down the river
they floated.

"Hooray!" the men shouted. Then the dinner
bell rang. "Time to eat." Paul led the way.

The men laughed and talked as they sat down
at the long tables. The cooks strapped on their
roller skates and picked up the huge platters full
of food. Up and down the room they skated.

"That's strange." Flapjack Freddy tapped Paul on the elbow. "I can't find Johnny."

Paul looked down the table. There was only an empty chair where the bookkeeper usually sat.

"Where is Johnny?" Paul asked.

"He was in a tree the last time I saw him," said Bart.

"He curled up in a hole to keep warm," another lumberjack said.

"A hole? In a tree?" The men looked at Paul. Paul looked at them. Johnny was in one of the trees floating down the river! He would go over the waterfall!

Paul and his men ran to the riverbank. "We'll never catch up to those logs."

"Come here, Babe," Paul Bunyan called to his big blue ox. When Babe came near, he whispered in her ear. Babe leaned over the river and began to drink. She drank and drank and drank. At last the river was empty. Only the muddy bottom of the riverbed was left. Far down the riverbed they could see the piled up logs. Paul began to run. The mud pulled at his boots with every step he took. When he reached the logs, the men lost sight of him. At last he returned, but where was Johnny?

The men sank down on the riverbank and put their heads in their hands. Paul reached into his pocket. He brought out Johnny, still curled up and still asleep!

A happy roar burst from the men. Johnny blinked and sat up. "What happened?" He looked around. "Where is the river?"

"Wait and see." Paul twisted the pipe of the cook house stove. Then he blew and blew until the stove glowed red hot. It melted the snow all around the river.

The water ran down the banks and filled up the riverbed. Again down the river floated ten thousand logs—no, it was nine thousand, nine hundred, ninety-nine. Paul couldn't charge the sawmill owner for the hollow log. After all, it could never be said that Paul Bunyan cheated.

White Silence

Eileen M. Berry

Last night while I slept,
the snow crept
on tiptoe
past my window,
silent as a dream.

When I awoke today,
the world lay
under sheets
with lumps and pleats,
white as whipped cream.

The trees around our place
were wearing lace
like bridal veils
from storybook tales
when I went out;

And the valley was so still
from hill to hill
that I whispered
to a red bird,
and it seemed a shout.

Noodle Soup

Gloria Repp /
illustrated by John Roberts

Part I

This summer we moved to the city. I missed feeding the chickens and hunting for Indian arrowheads and fishing in the creek. But I liked the city.

Trucks rumbled down our street. People hurried past our door. Everyone seemed to live in tall buildings that stretched up to the sky. And the lights stayed on all night.

Our apartment was small, but I had a bedroom all to myself. And I knew I'd never get tired of riding up and down in the elevator.

Fidget—my cat—prowled and meowed through every room before she settled down to sleep.

Lizz and Bett—the twins—laughed when they saw the playground. They ran from the swings to the slides to the jungle gym, and they made friends with everyone.

I don't know how much Mom liked the city.
But I knew she was happy that Dad could work at
a bigger airport.

The first week she was gone a lot, looking for a
job. Then she was busy working at the new job
she found and painting the apartment.

She painted the twins' room yellow and drew
flowers on the walls. She painted my room blue
with little airplanes around the edge, and she
drew a helicopter on my shade.

But one day she stopped fixing things up; she stopped singing too. She used to make up songs about her work and sing them in a low, scratchy sort of voice. We teased her about those funny songs, but not anymore.

Then she got sick.

"Just a cold," she said at first.

"Just a bad cold," she said later.

She kept going to work every day, but she came home and coughed at night.

Dad was working the late shift that week.

"Jon, I need some medicine," Mom said, and she sent me to the drugstore. I was glad when the medicine stopped her cough, but she still looked sick.

Every night she came home from work and lay down on the sofa. When she got a little better, she sat by the window.

She didn't cook real meals anymore. Dad and I heated up cans of spaghetti or stew. She said she wasn't hungry.

After a while I got to know Skeet—he lives down the hall. We played ball in the alley and ate ice cream at the park and traded baseball cards. He showed me a good climbing tree behind the playground. We set up tin-can telephones, and we're going to build a tree house.

His brother took us to the zoo. We rode there on the subway and bought cotton candy and fed the monkeys. It was fun doing things with Skeet.

But every day when I came home, I saw Mom sitting by the window. I wondered what she was thinking about, sitting there. Why doesn't she eat some supper, I thought. Maybe we shouldn't have moved.

One day I ate lunch at Skeet's house. His mother likes kids, and she makes good cookies. She asked about Mom's job and Dad's job and where we used to live. Then she asked if Mom was still sick. I don't know how she knew about Mom.

"Mom's not getting well," I said. "She's never hungry."

Skeet grinned. "This soup would fix her up. It's my grandma's famous recipe—won her a bunch of prizes."

I looked at Skeet's mother. "Can I help you make some soup for my mom?"

The next thing I knew, Skeet and I were chopping up piles of stuff. I cut myself twice, but I figured the soup would be worth it.

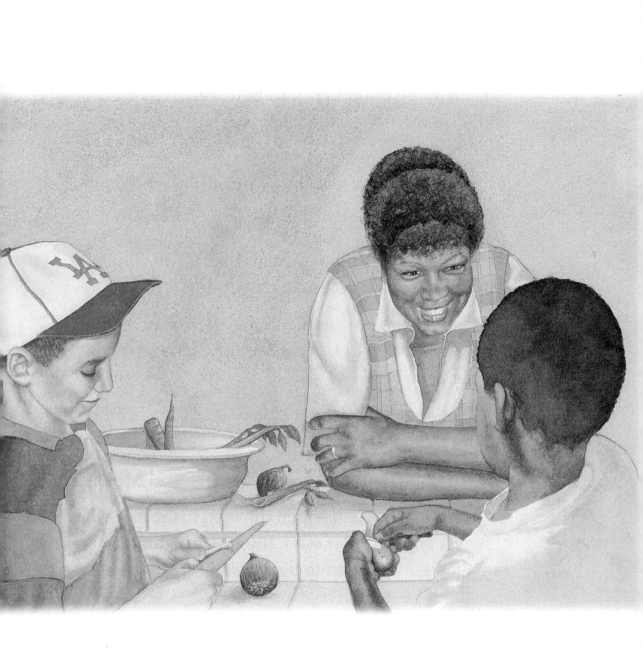

199

Part II

That night when Dad was working, we heard a knock at the door. Lizz and Bett were playing dolls on the floor, and Mom was sitting by the window.

Skeet's mother stood there, holding a big box.

"Hi, Mrs. Hart," said the twins.

She smiled. "Hello, Lizz and Bett. You climbed pretty high on that jungle gym today."

She put the box on the table. Then she went over and talked to Mom. She smiled at me when she left.

"Let's see what's in the box," cried Lizz and Bett. "Mom, can we open it?"

"You may look inside. Be careful," said Mom.

I helped the twins open the box. Inside was the biggest pot I've ever seen. It felt warm, and it smelled good. It had to be our soup.

201

Lizz and Bett took the lid off the pot. "Noodle soup!" they cried. "Can we have some?"

It looked like enough soup for the whole city. I spooned some of it into one of our little pots, and we ate it for supper.

That soup had carrots in it, and onions and celery, and chunks of real chicken; it had black speckles of pepper and bits of something green that Mom called parsley; and lots of noodles that floated on top.

Mom ate all of hers. Lizz and Bett and I had seconds. Fidget purred around my ankles until I dropped some chicken into her dish. And when Dad got home, he ate a bowl of soup too.

The next morning Mom ate some soup before she went to work.

"Noodle soup for breakfast?" I asked. I smiled at Dad, and he smiled back.

"It makes me feel warm inside," Mom said.

At supper time she had two bowls of soup and baked a frozen pizza for us. Later she talked on the phone to Mrs. Hart.

Mom ate soup again the next morning. That night she made us chili and cornbread, and she ate a piece of cornbread with the last of the soup. Then she scrubbed out the pot and took it over to Mrs. Hart. She was gone for a long time, but when she came home, she was smiling.

Tonight I heard Mom singing while she cooked our supper. It was a funny song about oodles of noodles, and it made us laugh.

I think Mom is getting well. Lizz and Bett say it's because of Mrs. Hart's soup. Maybe they're right.

But I don't think it was just the carrots and onions and celery and chunks of chicken and pepper and parsley and noodles floating on top.

I think it was something more.

Making Melody

The Nightingale

(adapted from a story by Hans Christian Andersen)

Becky Davis / illustrated by Tim Davis

A Plain Little Bird

Long ago in China there lived a mighty emperor who loved beautiful things. His gardens were full of the loveliest flowers in China. Little silver bells hung beside the flower beds. The bells rang gently when people walked by the flowers.

The Emperor's gardens stretched on and on until they led to a huge forest. At the edge of this forest there lived a nightingale.

The nightingale sang every night. He sang so sweetly that everyone who heard him would stop to listen.

People came from all over the world to admire the Emperor's palace and gardens. But when they heard the nightingale, they all decided that he was better than anything else they had seen or heard. Great people wrote stories and poems and even books about the lovely nightingale of China.

One day the Emperor of China received a book from the Emperor of Japan. It had been written about China. The emperor enjoyed all the parts that told about his palace and his gardens. "But the nightingale is the best," said the book.

The emperor called his most trusted servant. "Where is this nightingale? Why haven't I heard about him? The things the book says about his song sound too wonderful to believe."

The servant looked surprised.

"I'm sorry, your Majesty, but I haven't heard of the nightingale either."

"I want him presented to me at once!" The Emperor waved his hands.

The servant bowed and hurried out of the room. All through the palace he ran, asking every lord and lady he met about the bird. But none of them had heard of the nightingale. He ran back to the Emperor. "Your Majesty, the nightingale must be a story that these writers made up."

"If that nightingale isn't here tonight, everyone will be sent to bed without supper!" The Emperor was very angry.

This time all the court searched for someone who knew about the nightingale, because they didn't like the idea of going to bed without supper. At last, one little kitchen maid was found who had heard the bird.

"Oh, yes, the nightingale can sing gloriously," she said. "I pass him at the edge of the forest when I go home each night. Sometimes he even comes when I call him and lights on my finger."

"Little kitchen maid," said the servant, "please find that nightingale for us."

So the kitchen maid led the way, and the people of the court followed. On the way they heard a cow mooing.

"Oh, that's the nightingale!" They all stood still. "What a strong voice it has."

"No, no," said the kitchen maid. "That's just a cow. We're still far away from the nightingale."

As they walked farther, they heard a frog croaking. "How beautiful!" The court musician stopped to listen. "Is that the nightingale?"

"No, that's just a frog." The kitchen maid walked on. "But we may hear the nightingale soon." As the girl spoke, the nightingale began to sing. "There he is!" She pointed to the little brown bird.

"Oh, my!" All the court looked at the little bird. "To think that such a tiny, plain-looking bird could sing such a lovely song!" For a while they just stood and listened.

"Little girl, call the nightingale down to light on your finger." The chief servant pointed at the bird. "We must take him to the Emperor."

The nightingale lighted on the kitchen maid's finger and sang all the way back to the palace. "Oh, what a lovely song." All the court attendants agreed.

At the palace the nightingale sang so sweetly that tears came to the Emperor's eyes. "We will give the nightingale his own cage," he said.

So from that night on the nightingale lived at the palace. He could go outside twice a day, but twelve servants went with him, each holding a ribbon tied to the bird's legs. The poor nightingale didn't enjoy this at all.

One day the Emperor received a box labeled "The Nightingale."

"Oh, it must be another book about our famous bird." The Emperor opened the box with delight.

Inside the box there was a bird. But it wasn't a real bird. It was made of gold and silver, with jewels of all kinds on its wings and tail. A ribbon hung on its neck that said, "The Emperor of Japan's nightingale is better than the Emperor of China's nightingale."

The Best Song

When the golden nightingale was wound up, it sang a lovely song that was much like the song the real nightingale sang. While it sang, its tail moved up and down, glistening with silver and gold.

All the court listened. "How pretty! The two birds must sing together."

But that didn't work at all, for the real nightingale sang in one way and the golden nightingale sang in another way. So the Emperor decided they would listen to the golden bird sing alone again.

Everyone thought the song was just as lovely as the real nightingale's. And they all agreed that the new bird was much prettier to look at than the plain brown bird.

The golden nightingale sang the same song thirty-three times and it didn't get tired. The people wanted to hear it again, but the Emperor stopped them.

"We'll hear the real nightingale sing now," he
said.

But no one could find the real nightingale. He
had flown out the window and back to the forest
he loved.

"What an ungrateful bird!" The people of the
court were angry. "But we still have the best one."

And the golden nightingale was wound to sing
the same song once more.

The court musician praised the bird. "You can never tell what the real nightingale is going to sing, but we know ahead of time what this bird will do. We can even open it up and show others how it works. Your Majesty, this bird is far better than the real nightingale."

"Just what we thought!" The whole court clapped for the bird.

The real nightingale was banished from the empire, and the golden one was given a place of great respect. Long books were written about it, telling how wonderful it was.

And so a whole year passed. Everyone in the kingdom learned the golden nightingale's song, and this was the very reason they loved it so much.

But one evening when the Emperor lay in bed listening to the golden nightingale's song, he heard something unusual. "Whirr, clack, clack."

The Emperor sat up to look. The bird was twisting, and then it stopped with a "twang"!

"It's broken!" The Emperor called the court watchmaker.

The watchmaker fixed the bird, but he said that it must be treated very carefully because its gears were wearing out. The Emperor declared that the golden nightingale could be played only once a year.

And so five whole years went by. But then a sad thing happened. The Emperor got very sick. All the people of the court were sure he was about to die.

The Emperor lay in his great golden bed. He tossed and turned, shaking from his fever.

"Little golden nightingale, sing for me." He held his hand out to the golden bird. "Please sing to drive my fever away!" But the golden nightingale didn't move.

The night was fearfully quiet.

Suddenly through the silence, a lovely song filled the room. It was the real nightingale, perched on a branch outside the Emperor's window!

"Oh, little nightingale, you came back to me." The Emperor lay very still, listening to the nightingale's song. The lovely song brought sweet thoughts to his mind. He thought of the garden where the roses bloomed and the silver bells tinkled. He thought of the cool green forest where the breezes blew. As he lay quietly thinking of these pleasant things, he began to feel better.

"Little nightingale, I banished you from my kingdom, and you still came back to help me get well. How can I ever thank you?"

The little brown bird flicked his tail and sang even more sweetly.

"I understand," said the Emperor. "You don't want to be kept in a cage. Little nightingale, you may be free to fly around your green forest. But please sing at my window every night."

The nightingale bobbed his little head as if he understood. Then he sang a song that helped the Emperor sleep. Oh, what a sweet, refreshing sleep that was!

The next morning the servants came in, expecting to find their Emperor still very sick. Instead, he stood up and greeted them with a smile. "The nightingale—the *real* nightingale—sang a song that helped me get well. His music is the best an emperor could ever want."

The Flag Goes By

Henry Holcomb Bennett
illustrated by Paula Cheadle

Hats off!
Along the street there comes
A blare of bugles, a ruffle of drums,
A flash of color beneath the sky:
Hats off!
The flag is passing by!

Blue and crimson and white it shines,
Over the steel-tipped, ordered lines.
Hats off!
The colors before us fly!

O Say, Can You See?

Milly Howard / illustrated by Jim Harris (based on historical research)

In Enemy Hands

Francis Scott Key walked back and forth along the deck of the wooden ship. The breeze blowing off the Chesapeake Bay felt cool in the August heat, but Key did not notice.

"Can we go faster?" he asked as he stopped beside the captain and Colonel Skinner. "We must catch up to the British fleet. Dr. Beanes is in British hands! "

"We're going as fast as we can, sir," answered the captain. "Dr. Beanes is a friend of yours, isn't he?"

Mr. Key nodded. "Yes, he is. When I heard he had been arrested, I went to see President Madison. He said that Colonel Skinner and I could try to get the doctor released."

"Yes," said the colonel. "I brought some letters from British soldiers. They tell how Dr. Beanes helped them. The doctor was kind enough to treat the wounded on both sides of a battle."

"Look!" The captain pointed ahead. "There is the British fleet now."

Mr. Key leaned on the rail. "They are coming back this way!" he said. "I'm glad we're flying the truce flag!"

The other two men came to stand beside him. Nearly forty years ago, the American people had won a war against the British. Now the British and Americans were enemies in another war, which had begun two years earlier in 1812.

"There are over forty ships," said the captain. "The British admiral has joined another fleet of ships."

"So that is why they are coming back." The colonel frowned. "Now he has enough ships to attack Fort McHenry!"

The men watched the long line of ships come closer.

"There is the flagship." The captain pointed to one of the larger battleships.

"Hello," called the colonel to the men on board the flagship. "May we come aboard?"

Soon the answer came back. "Yes."

The captain watched as they rowed to the flagship and were helped aboard. Hours passed.

Victory at Dawn

From time to time the captain left his cabin to look up at the huge flagship. At last he heard voices, then the rattle of oars. The rowboat thumped against the side of the ship. The captain helped three men back on board. "You must be Dr. Beanes," he said, shaking the third man's hand.

"Yes," Dr. Beanes said, smiling. "The letters helped the admiral decide to release me." Then his smile disappeared. "But we are all prisoners until the battle at Fort McHenry is over."

"I was afraid of that," said the captain. "If they let us go now, we could tell the people at the fort about the attack."

The sky was dark as the little ship sailed with the British ships into the harbor.

Silently the men watched the busy sailors prepare for battle.

At last the harbor was quiet and still. The dark line of ships waited.

"Fire!" came the command from the flagship. A cannon roared. Then the other ships began firing across the harbor.

The men stared into the
darkness. Then as a rocket
exploded above the fort, they saw the
Stars and Stripes flying. "The flag is still there!"
Dr. Beanes shouted. "The fort has not fallen yet!"

All night Mr. Key paced the deck of the little
ship. From time to time he could see the flag.
Then, just before dawn, the noise stopped.

"Is the flag still there?" The men peered into the darkness, but they could see nothing. Not a sound disturbed the strange quiet. At last the sky began to glow with the early morning light. Patches of fog and smoke lifted for a moment. The men could barely see the flagpole above the fort.

"The flag?" asked Mr. Key.

Something fluttered on the flagpole. Then the torn flag could be seen waving in the morning breeze.

"The flag is still there!" Mr. Key cried as the captain and his crew cheered. "The flag is still there!"

Reaching for a piece of paper, Francis Scott Key began to write:

> O say, can you see, by the dawn's early
>   light,
> What so proudly we hailed at the
>   twilight's last gleaming?
> Whose broad stripes and bright stars,
>   through the perilous fight,
> O'er the ramparts we watched, were so
>   gallantly streaming!
> And the rockets' red glare, the bombs
>   bursting in air,
> Gave proof through the night that our
>   flag was still there:
> O say, does that star-spangled banner
>   yet wave
> O'er the land of the free and the home of
>   the brave?

Song of Faith

(based on II Chronicles 20:1-30)

Becky Davis / illustrated by Del Thompson

A Worried King

"Armies? Armies coming to fight us?"
The whispers spread through all the country of
Judah. "Armies have not tried to fight us for
years! Why would they come now?"

Worried people came out of their houses
to talk with each other. "Let's go to Jerusalem,"
some suggested. "We need to help the king."
Everywhere people got ready to leave for the
capital city.

The fathers said, "Bring enough water for the trip. The road is long, and the sun is hot."

The mothers said, "Come, come, children. Leave your toys and games. Hold on to our hands. We do not want you getting lost in the crowd."

Servants and masters, men and women, old and young, all left their houses and traveled to Jerusalem. The road overflowed with people.

In Jerusalem King Jehoshaphat sat in the palace, thinking and praying. He knew that the people of Judah were worried about the invading armies. He bowed his head in prayer. "Lord, please show me what to do."

A messenger entered the room and knelt before the king. "Your majesty, all the people of Judah are gathered together. They are standing outside waiting for you to speak."

"That is good," answered the king. "I want to talk to the Lord where all the people can hear me. They need to pray too."

The messenger left. King Jehoshaphat went to the temple to stand before all the people.

Men stopped arguing about the armies. Women stopped talking with each other. Boys and girls stopped playing. Everyone wanted to hear what the king would say.

Jehoshaphat cleared his throat and spoke to God. "Oh, Lord," he began, "You are the God that we serve. No one is as strong and powerful as You. You helped us to drive our enemies out of this land. And now, Lord, the wicked people of Moab and Ammon are coming to fight against us. Please judge them, because we are powerless against them. We do not know what to do, but we look to You for help."

All the people silently prayed with Jehoshaphat. When his prayer ended, they remained silent, praying in their hearts. The stillness was broken by the voice of one man. "Listen to me, O King, and all you people of Judah. The Lord has given me the answer." The man pressed through the crowd to reach the king. People whispered to each other, "Who is he?"

"I think he is Jahaziel," others answered. "He is a godly man. God must have spoken to him. He has something to tell us."

When Jahaziel came to the front, everyone became quiet again. "People of Judah," he began, "we will not have to fight as we usually do. The Lord is with us. He will fight for us. All we have to do is watch!"

The Singing Army

Jehoshaphat listened closely to what Jahaziel said. "Do you mean that we will not have to fight at all?" he asked.

"That is right," answered Jahaziel. "God has told me that tomorrow morning everyone should go down to the valley. That is where the enemy will be. You do not need to take any armor with you. The Lord will do all the fighting."

Jehoshaphat and all the people of Judah could hardly believe what they heard. At first the people murmured. But then Jehoshaphat kneeled to worship the Lord. Then they knelt too, worshiping the Lord.

Then Jahaziel and some other people stood up and began to sing. As loudly as they could, they all sang choruses of praise and glory to God. "Give thanks to the Lord, for His mercy is great," they sang.

"Worship him for His lovingkindness." All the
people listened to the beautiful music. God
listened too, and He was pleased.

"That is what we will do!" cried the king.
"Tomorrow morning we will go to the valley to
wait for the Lord to fight our battle for us. We will
have no spears or shields. We will have no bows
and arrows. But we will not stand quietly. We will
sing, giving God the glory for the great victory He
will give us."

236

The people cheered. Everyone was sure of the great victory they would have the next day.

Early in the morning all the people of Judah gathered together in the valley just as King Jehoshaphat had told them. They didn't talk loudly, but excitement was in the air.

King Jehoshaphat stood to get their attention. "Listen, people of Judah. Believe the Lord your God. Believe His prophets, and our nation will always be strong."

Then the king chose the ones that he knew were the very best singers. "You lead the people in singing praises to the Lord," he instructed.

And so they marched, without swords, spears, or shields. The singers sang their song beautifully. "Praise the Lord, for His mercy endureth forever." Their song echoed against the great hills surrounding the valley.

A messenger came running up. "King Jehoshaphat!" he cried. "I saw the enemy armies. It looked as though they were fighting each other!"

The king smiled, and the singers sang their song more loudly than ever. "Praise the Lord, for His mercy endureth forever."

At last the people came to the watchtower in the wilderness. Some men climbed up to see what they could see. The whole valley was quiet. Not a sound could be heard. "All the enemy armies have killed each other!" the men shouted.

"God is faithful!" cried King Jehoshaphat. "We didn't have to fight at all. God has given us the victory!"

What joyful singing there was when the people returned to Jerusalem! "Praise the Lord, for His mercy endureth forever," they all sang.

And God listened to them. And He was pleased.

Obedience

(a true story)

Ruth Greene and Susan W. Young
illustrated by Paula Cheadle

Five-year-old Becky Greene snuggled down into the seat between Dad and Mom. Her five brothers and sisters were each telling what they had learned at the revival meeting that night. When they stopped talking, Becky tapped Dad on the arm.

"I learned something tonight too, Daddy," she said.

"What did you learn, Becky?" Mr. Greene smiled.

Becky sat up tall. "I learned that I am supposed to do everything you and Mother tell me to do."

"That's a good thing." Mrs. Greene patted Becky's knee.

"But that's not all." Becky leaned closer to Mommy. "I'm supposed to do it when you say to do it."

"Is that so?" Mr. Greene grinned.

"Oh Daddy, you know that." Becky loved it when Daddy teased. "But I'm also supposed to do what you say with a 'happy' on my face."

"A 'happy' on your face?" Rick leaned up. "What does that mean?"

"Oh, Rick, it means obey right away with a happy face," answered Becky.

"Yes, that is what it means." Mrs. Greene looked back at the other children. "We all need to remember what Becky learned tonight. We all need to obey right away and with a 'happy' on our face."

Everyone laughed and agreed.

Several months later, the Greenes were traveling to North Carolina from their home in Michigan.

"Let's sing to pass the time," Mrs. Greene said as they started out.

Soon they had sung all the songs they liked best.

"What will we sing now, Mom?" Susan put her arms on the back of the seat. "We've sung all the songs we know."

Josh rubbed his throat. "Maybe we should just rest."

"Or maybe we should make up our own song," Mr. Greene said.

"What could we sing about?" Susan asked.

"You know," Mr. Greene stopped at a stop light. "People remember ideas that are put to music. Why don't we take the ideas from Becky's lesson that we use so often and put them to music."

"I would like that." Becky bounced in the seat.

"Becky's lesson would make a good song about obedience," Mrs. Greene said.

"But where do we start?" Cheryl pulled Susan back and leaned up. "We've never written a song before."

"Well, there's a verse in I John that talks about knowing what we believe by our obedience to God." Mr. Greene glanced back. "See if you can find that verse."

The car was quiet except for the turning of pages.

"Here it is!" Susan held up her Bible. "I John 2:3. 'And hereby we do know that we know Him, if we keep His commandments.' "

"That's it." Dad smiled into the rearview mirror. "Now what does that mean?"

"Keeping His commandments is obedience, isn't it?" Rick said. "So why don't we spell *obedience* as part of the song?"

"How's this?" Mr. Greene sang. "O-B-E-D-I-E-N-C-E."

"Obedience is the very best way to show that you believe." Mrs. Greene finished the tune.

"That's great!" All the children agreed.

"But how are we going to remember it?" Becky tugged on her mother's sleeve.

"We'll tape it and then we won't forget." Mrs. Greene reached under the seat for the tape recorder. Mr. and Mrs. Greene sang the song again.

"Now we need another part, one that says what obedience means," Susan said.

"We could write a verse that explains Becky's lesson," Mrs. Greene said. "Let's work together on it."

The family tried singing different words to a tune and then changed the tune to fit the words. Finally, they had recorded the new song on the tape.

The children sang the new song over and over again. Soon they had added another verse to the song. God used the lesson learned by little Becky Greene to give people a song that reminds them to be obedient to Him.

Obedience

Mike and Ruth Greene

Mike and Ruth Greene

1. O - bed - i - ence is the ver - y best way to show that you be - lieve.
2. We want to live pure, we want to live clean, we want to do our best;

Do - ing ex - act - ly what the Lord com - mands, Do - ing it hap - pi - ly.
Sweet - ly sub - mit - ting to au - thor - i - ty, Leav - ing to God the rest.

Ac - tion is the key, Do it im - med - i - ate - ly. Joy you will re - ceive. O -
Walk - ing in the light, keep - ing our at - ti - tude right, On the nar - row way; For

bed - i - ence is the ver - y best way to show that you be - lieve.
if we be - lieve the Word we re - ceive, we al - ways will o - bey.

Chorus

O - B - E - D - I - E - N - C - E, O -

bed - i - ence is the ver - y best way to show that you be - lieve.

Granny Nell's Dulcimer

Milly Howard

illustrated by John Roberts

The Dulcimer

For just a moment Tansy looked down at the
clear water and almost lost her balance. Her thin
arms waved in the air as she tried to keep from
falling. Then, putting one foot in front of the
other, she edged across the log.

247

"Whew! I thought I was going to fall in!" She let out her breath and sat down on a stump.

A blue jay chattered at her from a nearby tree. He seemed to be making fun of her.

"Oh, hush," Tansy said. "I know it's a small stream, but who wants to get wet!"

The bird hopped back and forth across the twig, scolding Tansy. Then he stopped, tilting his head to one side to listen. Faint music drifted down the trail.

"What's that?" Tansy whispered. She stood up and brushed off her skirt. As she crept up the trail, the music became louder. She pushed the leaves aside and stared at an old gray cabin. Tansy left her hiding place and moved quietly around the stone chimney. An old woman sat on the porch, holding an instrument in her lap. The woman plucked the strings with something that looked like a feather.

The music made Tansy think of sunshine and laughter and faraway places.

"Come here, child."

Tansy started as though she had been dreaming.

"Well, come on up here where I can get a look at you." The woman motioned her closer.

Tansy slowly climbed the steps and stood in front of the rocker.

"You must have come up the back way," said the woman. "Not many people use that trail nowadays. Do you live around here?"

"Yes, ma'am, we just moved back here," Tansy said.

"Folks around here call me Granny," the old woman said. The rocker creaked as she leaned back. "You must be Jim and Nora Ledford's daughter."

Tansy's eyes widened. "Tansy Ledford. How did you know?"

"I just guessed," said the woman. "You look like your mother did when she was about your age. I know your folks from way back. Ask your mother about old Granny Nell." She patted the rocker next to her. "Come and sit down."

Tansy pulled the rocker closer to Granny Nell and sat down. Granny slid a dried chicken bone up and down the strings of her instrument. With her right hand she plucked the strings with a turkey quill.

Granny played one song after another. Tansy discovered that she knew some of the tunes.

"Just watch," Granny said. She began to play a lively tune called "Turkey in the Straw." A tiny head popped out of the branches next to the porch. Then a squirrel scampered out on a limb. Tansy clapped her hands over her mouth to keep from laughing. The squirrel hopped up and down. It looked like he was keeping time with the music.

"Sh," warned Granny Nell. Tansy sat very still. Granny played "Pop Goes the Weasel." A flock of blue jays swooped down into the yard. They flew around the yard, diving at each other.

Tansy's eyes were bright with laughter when Granny Nell finally stopped playing. "Do they always come up when you play?" Tansy asked.

"I usually play the same time every day," Granny replied. "My little friends wouldn't know what to do without their afternoon music." She ran her fingers over the strings.

"What is that thing you're playing?" Tansy asked.

"A dulcimer," Granny replied. "An old-time dulcimer that belonged to my mother." She looked at the sun. "You had better be on your way before the sun sets. Come back tomorrow, and I'll show you how to play the dulcimer."

"Will you, for sure?" Tansy asked.

"Sure will," Granny replied. "Now scoot!"

Summer on Shady Mountain

All summer long Tansy climbed the back trail to Granny Nell's cabin. The noisy blue jay grew used to her visits. He no longer scolded Tansy when she ran across the log.

Tansy whistled at him happily. "Morning, Blue," she called as she hurried past his tree.

At the cabin Tansy found Granny in the kitchen making tea. "Take the dulcimer outside, Tansy. I'll be right out," she said.

"Play 'Church in the Wildwood,' Tansy," Granny said, sitting down in the other rocker. She tapped her foot in time to the music. Granny nodded to herself as the notes faded. "I've never had anyone learn to play the dulcimer as fast as you have. The good Lord has given you a gift, Tansy. Make sure you use it well."

"But the animals don't come when I play," said Tansy.

"Give them time," Granny said, smiling. "They'll come around soon enough."

"Mother says that you play at the Shady Mountain Fair," Tansy said. "She says you always win the music competition."

Granny nodded. "So far I have. The extra money helps me to pay the taxes on my land."

She looked around her at the honeysuckle vines, heavy with sweet-smelling blossoms. Then she looked out across the valley to the blue-misted mountains.

"I hope I never have to leave my mountains," she said. Then she shook her head as if to clear it of gloomy thoughts. "Let's go for a walk before you go home," she said. Tansy took many more walks with Granny Nell. Each day Granny showed her something new about life on the mountain. One day it was a pale, speckled egg from a blue jay's nest. The next day it was a tiny wildflower almost hidden under the damp leaves.

One afternoon Tansy skipped up the trail and stopped by the log to watch the rushing water. Whistling for Blue as usual, she started across the log. On the other side she stopped and looked about her. There had been no cheerful answering whistle. Puzzled, she whistled again. There was a sudden flash of blue, and the little blue jay dashed about her head, scolding loudly.

"What's wrong with you?" Tansy asked, ducking her head. Blue just flew up the trail, still scolding.

"All right, I'm coming!" Tansy ran to keep up with him. "Granny Nell!" she called as she ran around the cabin.

Granny Nell was sitting in her rocker. She looked up, her face white with pain. "What's wrong?" Tansy stopped to catch her breath.

"I slipped on the way to the spring," said Granny. "I hit a rock when I fell; I think my arm is broken."

"I'll get Mother," said Tansy. "We'll bring the car back."

Mrs. Ledford was in the kitchen. Tansy ran into the house.

"What's wrong?" Mrs. Ledford asked.

"Granny's hurt!" Tansy called. "We need to take her to the doctor."

They drove over the bumpy, winding road to Granny's cabin. It took over an hour to get Granny to the clinic. Tansy and her mother waited until the doctor finished with Granny's cast.

"Now you'll stay with us for a few weeks," Mrs. Ledford said.

"Oh, no," said Granny. "I don't want to be a bother—"

"You won't be, Granny." Mrs. Ledford smiled. "You'll always be welcome in our home."

"Please, Granny," Tansy pleaded.

"All right," said Granny, slowly. "If you're sure I'll not be in the way."

"You won't be!" both Tansy and her mother answered.

Mountain Melodies

The next morning Tansy balanced a tray and knocked on Granny's bedroom door.

"Come in!"

Tansy pushed open the door.

"Let me help," said Granny, starting to get up.

"Wait, Granny," Tansy said. She walked across the room. "There, I made it!" she said. She set the tray down, being careful not to hit Granny's cast.

"Thank you, Tansy," said Granny. She handed Tansy a piece of buttered toast. "Now you can help me eat all this." Tansy grinned. "Mother did give you a lot, didn't she?" She reached for a slice of bacon. Her hand stopped in midair. "Granny," she said. "You can't play in the contest with a broken arm!"

"No," Granny replied. "I can't play with one hand. But we do need the dulcimer. Ask your mother if you can go get it this morning."

Tansy frowned, still thinking about the contest. "But you need the money."

"Now, child," Granny said, "you get that worried look off your face. The Lord has always provided for me. Things have a way of working out when you trust Him."

"All right, Granny," Tansy said. "I'll go ask Mother if I can go now."

"I heard," Mother said as she knocked at the door. "You run along. I need to talk to Granny about something."

Tansy half ran, half walked up the trail. At the log she stopped and whistled for Blue.

Wings flashed in the sunlight as Blue landed on her finger.

"You've never come this close before," Tansy whispered. "You're worried, too, aren't you?"

Blue chirped and flew back up the trail.

Tansy followed. At the cabin, she took the dulcimer off the peg. As she started out the door, a tiny animal scampered out onto a limb.

"You miss your music, don't you? Granny Nell didn't get to play for you yesterday."

Tansy sat on the porch steps and played the songs Granny had taught her. The squirrel hopped closer, tilting his head to one side.

"So you finally like the way I play," said Tansy. It was then that the thought came to her. "I wonder if I could enter the contest," she said to the little squirrel. "If I win, I could give Granny the money for her taxes."

She held the dulcimer close and walked down the trail to her house.

"Mom, Granny," Tansy called. She stopped at the door of the spare room.

The two women looked up.

"I want to enter the music contest at the fair," Tansy said. "That is, if Granny will let me use her dulcimer."

"You may use the dulcimer, Tansy. But you need to play a lot," Granny said.

"I will every day!" said Tansy.

And so she did.

The Contest

Every day Tansy played and sang the old songs. Granny tapped her foot and sang along with her. The day of the contest came closer and closer.

At last Tansy found herself seated on the stage with the other contestants. She clutched the dulcimer tightly in her lap. One of the fiddlers leaned over and patted her on the arm.

"Relax," he said. "Just think of something that you really like and you'll do fine."

Tansy looked out across the crowd. Then the announcer's voice rose above the noise of the tuning instruments. "And now, our first contestant is Harley Stevens, playing the fiddle."

Soon even Tansy was tapping her foot to the lively music. Each player seemed better than the last. Then came the dreaded announcement: "Our last contestant, Tansy Ledford, is new to the dulcimer but was taught by the best, Granny Nell!"

Tansy rubbed her hands on her dress and walked to the front of the stage. She sat in the chair the announcer held for her. Then she drew the feather over the strings. At first the beating of her heart seemed louder than the music. Tansy closed her eyes so she wouldn't have to see the people.

Then as she played she thought of Blue's wings flashing in the summer sun. She thought of the smell of honeysuckle, of the light lavender scent in Granny's clothes, and of the smell of Mother's home-baked bread.

As the last notes of "Amazing Grace" faded, Tansy opened her eyes. The people were quiet. Then as Tansy returned to her seat, they called out "hurrah, hurrah." The announcer stood up. "All the contestants did a fine job," he began. Tansy held her breath. He finished his little speech, "And the winner is . . . Harley Stevens!"

Tansy let out her breath slowly. She hadn't won. Slowly she picked up the dulcimer and left the stage. Mother and Granny Nell met her at the steps.

Mother hugged her close. "You played beautifully, Tansy!" she said.

Harley Stevens stopped beside them. "You did a terrific job for such a young one." He turned to Granny. "It won't be long before she plays as well as you do, Granny Nell."

"I think so myself," Granny said proudly.

"But Granny," said Tansy, "I didn't win any money."

Granny put her good arm around Tansy. "Now don't you worry about that. Your mother wants you to have more lessons on the dulcimer. And she wants to pay me to be your teacher." She squeezed Tansy. "There's nothing I would like better!"

Tansy squeezed Granny back. "Me either, Granny!"

More About Dulcimers

Muriel Murr

illustrated by John Roberts

Jo and Rogers Magee have a dulcimer shop in the Appalachian Mountains. If you were to visit their shop, you would be welcomed by smiling faces and the sound of dulcimer music.

The Magees love children. They even help children make their own dulcimers from kits. Boys and girls enjoy making "The Hiker" dulcimer, which is a short instrument with only three strings. Can you guess why it is called "The Hiker"?

"The Hiker" is just the right size to sling over your back and carry with you on a hike. When you get tired of hiking, you can sit down and relax with some dulcimer playing.

How would you like to learn to make and play an instrument much like Tansy's mountain dulcimer? With a little help from a parent or teacher, making this instrument is not hard at all.

Mr. and Mrs. Magee invented an instrument that is easier to make than the three-stringed dulcimer. It has only one string, and it is called the OONEE-CAN. The can is what helps the sound to echo or vibrate. The can is attached to a long board called a *fret board*. The string runs the length of the fret board. But if there is only one string, how will the pitches change?

On the fret board are little metal strips, or *frets*. They are spaced out along the board to make a pattern of pitches called a *scale*.

Hold a craft stick in one hand. Press the string down between frets. Hold a guitar pick in your other hand. Gently strum it across the string and you're making a lovely sound.

Dulcimer music uses numbers to tell you which fret to press. So who can play the OONEE-CAN? Anyone can!

Psalm 33:1-3

Rejoice in the Lord, O ye righteous:
For praise is comely for the upright.
Praise the Lord with harp:
Sing unto him with the psaltery
And an instrument of ten strings.
Sing unto him a new song;
Play skilfully with a loud noise.

Fanny Crosby

Becky Davis and Eileen M. Berry
illustrated by Johanna Berg

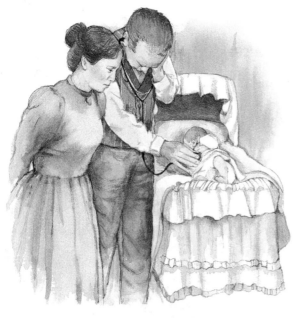

First Years

Fanny Crosby's mother bundled her up in a thick quilt. She rocked her back and forth until Fanny's eyes closed in sleep. Before long, a horse whinnied from the yard, and the doctor knocked at the door. Quickly, Mrs. Crosby led him to Fanny's cradle.

He listened to the baby's heartbeat. "How old is your little girl?" he asked.

"Just six weeks old," said Mrs. Crosby. "Will she be all right? She's had a bit of a cold, but now I'm worried about her eyes. They are red and swollen."

"I'll give you some medicine for her eyes," the doctor said. "She should be well shortly."

Mr. and Mrs. Crosby followed the doctor's directions closely, but Fanny's eyes did not heal. The medicine only made them worse. At last they knew that Fanny could no longer see.

As Fanny grew up, she did not let her blindness stop her from running and playing. She climbed trees, rode horseback, and romped through the fields by her home. With her fingers she learned to "see" everything—especially the face of her dear grandmother.

Grandmother taught Fanny about the beautiful world God had created. Fanny learned the names of the songbirds from Grandmother. When the birds perched on the trees to sing, Fanny listened until she knew their songs by heart.

Grandmother read the Bible to Fanny almost every day. Before long Fanny had memorized whole books of the Bible.

"Fanny," Mother said early one morning, "we're going to New York. Doctor Mott wants to look at your eyes. Maybe he will be able to help you see."

Even though she could not see, Fanny dressed herself. She put on her best dress and combed her hair.

All the way to New York, Fanny tried to sit quietly. But her feet kept tapping the floor of the train.

In New York loud noises on the streets frightened Fanny. She walked close to her mother.

Dr. Mott carefully checked Fanny's eyes. Then he slowly shook his head. "I'm afraid you will always be blind, Fanny," he said.

Sadly, Mrs. Crosby took Fanny home. Nothing else could be done.

Though she would never see, Fanny made up her mind to be happy. After her eighth birthday, she wrote a poem:

> O what a happy soul am I,
> Although I cannot see,
> I am resolved that in this world
> Contented I will be.
> How many blessings I enjoy
> That other people don't!
> To weep and sigh because I'm blind
> I cannot and I won't.

Fanny continued to make up poems. And her grandmother kept on reading to her. Fanny carefully stored all she heard in her memory. A dream began in her heart.

"I wish I could go to school and learn like other children do," she thought.

One night after Grandmother had prayed with her, Fanny sat thinking about school and her blindness. She knew God answered prayer. She knelt by her bed. "Dear Lord, please show me how I can learn like other children."

Many days passed. One morning Fanny opened the gate to the front yard. She heard a paper rustle.

"Mother?" Fanny asked.

"Yes, Fanny, it's Mother. The mailman was just here. He brought a letter for you from the New York Institute for the Blind. Would you like to go to school?"

"School!" Fanny cried. "Oh, Mother, I want to go to school more than anything in the world."

New Sight

At the New York Institute for the Blind, Fanny learned to read Braille with her fingers. She studied English, arithmetic, and history. And she made friends.

More and more often she wrote poems. Since the class she liked best was music, she began singing some of her poems. Her new friends at the Institute joined her. Fanny enjoyed her friends and her studies so much that the years seemed to pass quickly.

When she grew up, she did not leave the school. She took a job as a teacher.

One Monday morning as she stood in front of the class, someone told her that one of the students was very ill. Fanny hurried to the student's room. The sick girl was too weak to sit up.

"Good-bye, Miss Crosby," she whispered.

The next morning the girl died.

The illness spread quickly. Fanny stopped teaching and became a nurse. One evening, she began feeling sick herself. "I don't want anyone to worry," Fanny thought. "I'll go to bed early. Maybe rest will help me." By the next morning she felt better.

But now Fanny was troubled. "If I had died from that illness," she thought, "would I have gone to heaven?" She had never asked Christ to save her.

One night at church Fanny knew what she had to do.

Right then Fanny asked the Lord to forgive her sins and be her Savior.

Now Fanny wanted to write all of her poems for the Lord.

She remembered the Bible stories her grandmother had read to her. She wrote—

Tell me the story of Jesus,
Write on my heart every word.
Tell me the story most precious
Sweetest that ever was heard.

281

A new teacher named Al Van Alstyne came to the Institute. Mr. Van Alstyne was blind too. He had been a student at the Institute years before, and now he had returned to teach music.

Mr. Van Alstyne liked Fanny's poems. Sometimes he wrote music for them. And Fanny liked the music Mr. Van Alstyne wrote. The two teachers became good friends.

One day Mr. Van Alstyne asked Fanny to marry him. Fanny did not have to think about her answer for very long. She left her teaching job to become Mr. Van Alstyne's wife.

Since she did not teach, Fanny had more time to write. Her husband wrote music for more of her poems. Many became gospel songs that people in churches across America and in England sang.

Fanny often thanked the Lord for helping her write. One of her songs says—

> This is my story,
> This is my song,
> Praising my Savior
> All the day long.

Fanny never grew tired of praising the Lord in song. By the end of her life she had written eight thousand gospel songs.

Though she lived in darkness because she was blind, she wanted to show others the light of God's Word. Once people were saved, they could sing with her—

> Redeemed, how I love to proclaim it,
> Redeemed by the blood of the Lamb.
> Redeemed through his infinite mercy
> His child and forever I am.

"Fanny," a preacher said to her, "it is too bad that God did not give you the gift of sight."

Fanny smiled. "Not so! Just think, the first face I will ever see will be the face of Christ my Savior. I believe God intended that I should be blind so that I could praise Him better. If I had my sight, I might never have written my poems."

When Fanny was ninety-four years old, she went home to be with the Lord. She had written about heaven many years before—

And I shall see Him face to face,
And tell the story saved by grace.

The Song of Happy People

Gail Fitzgerald / illustrated by
Stephanie True and John Bjerk

Clinkety-clank, clinkety-clank. The baker's new pans went clinkety-clank.

Tippety-tap, tippety-tap. The shoemaker's hammer went tippety-tap.

Swishety-swoosh, swishety-swoosh. The weaver's long reeds went swishety-swoosh.

All the people in town were busy making music as they worked—everyone except Mr. McDoogle. He was much too old to work. Every day he sat on his porch and patted his bony knee in time to the clank of the baker's new pans, the tap of the shoemaker's hammer, and the swoosh of the weaver's long reeds. He never missed a beat.

"Ah," he would say, leaning back in his old chair. "The song of happy people at work is a good song."

Then one day a stranger crept into town. His dark suit blended in well with the shadows. Only Mr. McDoogle saw him creeping down Main Street, glancing this way and that.

"That man is up to no good," Mr. McDoogle said to himself. "He need not think that he will get into my house."

The stranger pushed open the door to the baker's shop, letting the clinkety-clank of the baker's pans float down the street.

"Good morning, stranger," said the baker, clapping his hands together until clouds of flour flew around.

"What's good about it?" the stranger grumbled. "It's too chilly outside. Your rolls might not rise on a day like this."

The baker scratched his nose. Then he sat down on a stool. "What will I do if my rolls won't rise?" he asked.

"Close up shop till the air is just right," said the stranger. Then he slipped out the door. The baker followed him, locking the door as he went.

The stranger hurried quickly down the street. Into the shoemaker's shop he went, letting the tippety-tap of the shoemaker's hammer float down the street.

"Good morning, stranger," said the shoemaker, jumping up and scattering tacks into the cracks of the floor.

"What's good about it?" the stranger muttered. He shook his head. "Times are bad, bad, bad. Everything costs too much. And now you might not have the tacks you need to finish the job."

The shoemaker looked into the almost empty pockets of his apron and sighed. "What will I do if I don't have the tacks I need?"

"Close up shop till prices come down," said the stranger. Then he vanished out the door. The shoemaker followed him, locking the door as he went.

The stranger lost no time in making his way to the weaver's shop. The bell tinkled as he pushed open the door. The swishety-swoosh of the weaver's long reeds floated into the air.

"Good morning, stranger," said the weaver, stepping on a brittle reed and snapping it in two.

"What's good about it?" the stranger growled. "You just broke a reed. All of your reeds might be too brittle to make baskets."

The weaver's brown eyes opened wide. "What should I do if my reeds are too brittle?" he cried.

The stranger shrugged. "Better close up shop. You might never have soft reeds." He scuttled out the door. The weaver followed him, locking the door as he went.

The stranger started back up Main Street. Behind him came the baker, wringing his hands. Behind the baker came the shoemaker, twisting his apron. Behind the shoemaker came the weaver, biting his fingernails. No one was making music because no one was working. No one was working because everyone was thinking, "What if. . . ."

Right up to Mr. McDoogle's house they went. Mr. McDoogle was sitting on his porch, but his hand was not patting his bony knee. "Something is not right," he called out. "I do not hear the song of happy people anymore. I don't hear the clinkety-clank of the baker's new pans or the tippety-tap of the shoemaker's hammer or the swishety-swoosh of the weaver's long reeds."

"But what if my rolls won't rise . . ."

"Or I do not have the tacks I need . . ."

"Or my reeds are too brittle?"

"Plan your work and work your plan," said old Mr. McDoogle. "Do what you have to do to get the job finished. And remember," he said, pointing to the stranger slinking out of sight, "fear is never a good friend."

The baker clapped his hands. "I can let my rolls rise in a warm oven."

The shoemaker snapped his fingers. "I can pick up the tacks I spilled."

The weaver put his hands on his hips. "I can soak my brittle reeds in water till they are soft."

The three friends set off down Main Street, singing happily. And old Mr. McDoogle leaned back in his chair, patting his bony knee in time to the song of happy people.

When Singing Came Again

Eileen M. Berry
illustrated by Mary Ann Lumm

The Instrument

Our island is full of music. Sea birds cry in
long, lonely notes above the quiet beaches. In the
streets the steel bands play, tapping out their
tinny tunes on oil drums. The sea itself is music—
a faraway rumble when I lie in bed or a whistling
roar held close to my ear in a big pink shell.

And our people sing. The farmers sing in the sugar cane fields. The fishermen sing in their smelly boats. The ladies in the market stalls sing out their wares. "Bracelets of pretty beads! Baskets made from palm leaves! Coconuts! Mangoes!" Their voices rise and fall in eager calls.

Music sings around me every day—all around the house where I live with my mama and papa and two brothers. Sometimes there is music inside the house too. We sing the island songs. We sing the songs from the hymnbook at church. We all sing together, but Mama sings loudest. Mama is the one who taught us to sing.

I remember the day that my baby sister arrived. My brothers and I sang her a welcome song that we made up ourselves. Mama stood beside her crib and very softly sang her to sleep.

But then something happened to stop all the singing. My baby sister died. For many days after that, there was no music in our house.

On one of these silent mornings, Mama handed me the big yellow basket. "Vanessa, I need you to go to market for coconuts," she said.

I ran with the basket over roads my bare feet knew well.

I had not gone far when I heard music. It was different from the steel band music. It was different from the music I heard at church. The notes were high and clear. The tune was cheerful.

I turned beside a bright pink bougainvillea bush. I followed the music to the door of a little house.

A boy in ragged clothes was sitting on the step. He held a piece of metal to his mouth. As he blew into it, he moved it back and forth and music played. Behind him, just inside the door, a baby lay on a blanket. She wiggled and waved her tiny arms.

"Hello," I said.

The boy stopped playing and smiled. "Hello."

"I heard your music from the road." I tipped my head. "I live just back that way. What's that you're blowing on?"

"Harmonica," he said, holding the piece of metal up for me to see. He lifted it again, and in one blow he played two notes together.

"It's nice," I said.

He smiled again and pointed to the baby. "My sister likes the music," he said. "I'm keeping her quiet for Mama." He leaned toward me. "Mama feels very bad. She's been sick for a week."

I peered into the dark little room behind him. In the dim light I could see a woman in bed. "Is there anyone to help you?" I asked.

He shook his head. "It is just us three," he said. He began to play again.

I stood and listened for a while. "I have to go to market," I said.

I came back home with the coconuts. While Mama cooked rice and peas in coconut milk, I told her about the boy.

"Please, Mama," I said. "Can we go back to see them today?"

Mama's mouth was set in a certain way, and I knew she would not answer right then. "We will see," she said.

After lunch I watched to see what Mama would do. She picked up her Bible and went outside. My brothers and I played a game with shells and beans.

Mama returned much later. She laid her Bible on the table and picked up the basket. She went into the back room where we kept the baby crib. Then she went into the kitchen. She came back and stood over me.

"Let's go, Vanessa," she said.

I jumped up. "To market again?"

"No." She smiled just a little. "To the boy's house."

The Gift

I led Mama down the road, trying hard not to break into a run. "What's in the basket, Mama?" I asked.

"Just a few things," Mama said. "A few things I thought they might need."

Soon we heard the music again. "It's a harmonica, Mama," I said. "Isn't it nice?"

"Yes, Vanessa, it's very nice."

I looked for the bougainvillea bush. "This is the house," I said.

The boy still sat on the steps. This time the baby was asleep. Mama looked first at the boy, then at the baby.

"What is your name, little man?" she asked the boy.

He sat up straight. "My name is Marcus," he said. "Did you come to see my mama? She's in bed today."

"I came to leave you some things," Mama said.

Marcus lifted the cloth that covered the basket. I leaned close to see. Inside was a bowl of leftover rice and peas from our lunch. Beside the bowl was a pile of coconuts and bananas. Marcus's eyes grew big.

"So much food!" he said. "My mama will be very happy. Thank you."

Mama stooped down and lifted the coconuts and bananas out, one by one. She set the bowl on the steps. I saw that there was a second layer in the basket.

Mama pulled back another cloth. I gasped.

Three piles of folded clothes lay in the bottom of the basket. Little dresses, tiny shirts, doll-sized skirts, and even fancy stockings. "Mama!" I said. "Those were for—"

"Hush, Vanessa," Mama said. She turned to me and put her finger to her lips. Her mouth was set in that certain way again. I was silent.

"Your sister will need these things," Mama told Marcus. "We do not need them. Please give them to your mama."

Marcus stood up. "I'll go tell her now," he said.

"Wait," said Mama. "One more thing. Tell your mama I will be back tomorrow. I will bring more food. I will clean the house. Vanessa will come and mind the baby."

Marcus ran into the dark room. A minute later, he came back. "Mama says thank you," he said. "And please—take this."

He handed me the harmonica. I looked up at Mama. She nodded her head just a little.

"Thank you," I said. "Tomorrow, you will teach me to play?"

Marcus nodded.

All the way home, I tried to play the harmonica. It squeaked and squealed in funny sounds.

Mama laughed her rich, deep laugh. "Give up, child," she said. "I have a better idea." And she began to sing.

From that day on, there was singing again in our house.

Glossary

This glossary has information about selected words found in this reader. You can find meanings of words as they are used in the stories. Certain unusual words such as foreign names are included so that you can pronounce them correctly when you read.

The pronunciation symbols below show how to pronounce each vowel and several of the less familiar consonants.

ă	pat	ĕ	pet	îr	fierce
ā	pay	ē	be	ŏ	pot
âr	care	ĭ	pit	ō	go
ä	father	ī	pie	ô	paw, for, ball

oi	oil	ŭ	cut	zh	vision
o͝o	book	ûr	fur	ə	ago, item,
o͞o	boot	*th*	the		pencil, atom,
yo͞o	abuse	th	thin		circus
ou	out	hw	which	ər	butter

A

admiral

anemone

ă	pat	ĕ	pet
ā	pay	ē	be
âr	care	ĭ	pit
ä	father	ī	pie
îr	fierce	oi	oil
ŏ	pot	o͝o	book
ō	go	o͞o	boot
ô	paw,	yo͞o	abuse
	for	ou	out
ŭ	cut	ə	ago,
ûr	fur		item,
th	the		pencil,
th	thin		atom,
hw	which		circus
zh	vision	ər	butter

ad • mi • ral | ăd´ mər əl | The commander-in-chief of a fleet.

a • las | ə lăs´ | A word used to express sorrow, regret, or grief.

al • bi • no | ăl bī´ nō | A person or animal that does not have normal coloration. The skin and hair are completely white, and the eyes are usually red or blue.

a • nem • o • ne | ə něm´ ə nē | A sea animal with a flexible body shaped like a tube.

an • nounc • er | ə nouns´ sər | A person whose job is to speak to the public on radio, television, or over a public-address system.

ap • pa • la • chi • an | ăp´ ə lā´ chē ən | Anything that refers to a region of the northeastern United States, including the Appalachian Mountains.

a • pron | ā´ prən | A garment tied around the waist to keep a person's clothes clean.

aunt | ănt | or | änt | The sister of one's father or mother.

a • vaunt | ə vônt´ | or | ə vänt´ | To go away from a particular place.

B

bal • ance | băl´ əns | 1. A steady or stable position. 2. To hold in a steady or stable position.

ban • ish | băn´ ish | To force a person or thing to leave a place; to drive away.

be • decked | bĭ **dĕkd´** | Past tense and past participle of **bedeck:** To elaborately adorn someone or something.

black • smith | **blăk´** smĭth | A person who makes things out of iron.

bou • gain • vil • le • a | boo´ gən **vĭl´** ē ə | A woody shrub or vine native to South America. The bougainvillea is characterized by having groups of petal-like colored bracts attached to its flowers. Often the flowers are a distinctive shade of pink.

blacksmith

Braille | brāl | A system of writing and printing for blind people.

can • tan • ker • ous | kăn **tăng´** kər əs | Bad-tempered; having a tendency to quarrel.

bougainvillea

can • teen | kăn **tēn´** | A container for carrying drinking water or other liquids.

can • vas | **kăn´** vəs | A heavy, coarse cloth used for making tents, sails, etc.

car • a • mel | **kăr´** ə məl | A brown syrup made by cooking sugar; used to color and flavor foods.

char • i • ot | **chăr´** ē ət | A two-wheeled vehicle pulled by horses.

chariot

chil • i | **chĭl´** ē | A Mexican dish made with tomatoes, peppers, beans, hamburger, and spices.

clin • ic | **klĭn´** ĭk | A place that gives medical help to patients not staying in the hospital.

clink • e • ty | klǐngk´ ə tē | A word used to describe anything that makes a sharp ringing sound.

clothes | klōz | Coverings worn on the body.

cobblestone

cob • ble • stone | kŏb´ əl stōn´ | A round stone once used to cover streets.

col • ors | kŭl´ ərz | A flag or banner of a country or military unit.

com • mend • eth | kə mĕnd´ əth | Old way of writing or saying **commends:** To show to be desirable.

cour • age | kŭr´ ǐj | A quality of character that makes a person able to face danger or hardship without fear or in spite of fear.

court | kôrt | The attendants, advisors, and other people who work for a king.

cubbyhole

cov • er | kŭv´ ər | To place something over or upon.

crim • son | krǐm´ zən | A bright purplish-red color.

cub • by • hole | kŭb´ ē hōl´ | A small, snug area or room.

D **dan • ger** | dān´ jər | The chance or threat of something harmful happening.

dike | dīk | A wall, dam, or embankment built to hold back water and prevent flooding.

dike

dis • ci • ples | dǐ sī´ pəlz | The twelve chosen followers of Christ. The disciples helped to spread the teachings of Christ.

dis • cov • er | dĭ **skŭv´** ər | To find or come upon something for the first time.

em • per • or | **ĕm´** pər ər | A man who rules an empire.

emperor

en • dur • eth | ĕn **door´** əth | The old way of saying or writing **endures:** To put up with; stand; bear.

Eng • lish | **ĭng´** glĭsh | The language of Great Britain, the United States, Canada, Australia, and various other countries throughout the world.

es • pe • cial • ly | ĭ **spĕsh´** ə lē | 1. In a special way; more than usually; very. 2. More than others; particularly.

ă	pat	ĕ	pet
ā	pay	ē	be
âr	care	ĭ	pit
ä	father	ī	pie
îr	fierce	oi	oil
ŏ	pot	o͝o	book
ō	go	o͞o	boot
ô	paw,	yo͞o	abuse
	for	ou	out
ŭ	cut	ə	ago,
ûr	fur		item,
th	the		pencil,
th	thin		atom,
hw	which		circus
zh	vision	ər	butter

faint | fānt | Not clearly seen, sensed, or heard; weak.

fa • mous | **fā´** məs | Widely known; celebrated.

flan | flăn | or | flän | A Spanish dessert made with caramel.

flap • jack | **flăp´** jăk | A pancake.

flapjack

flour • ish | **flûr´** ĭsh | or | **flŭr´** ĭsh | To wave in a bold or showy way.

gal • lant • ly | **găl´** ənt lē | Bravely or courageously performed.

gears | gîrz | Plural of **gear:** A wheel with teeth around the edge that fit into the teeth of another wheel. Gears are used to send motion or power from one machine part to another.

gears

grid • dle | grĭd´ l | A flat metal surface or pan for cooking.

glow | glō | To give off a steady light.

gos • pel | gŏs´ pəl | The good news of salvation through Jesus Christ.

 hail | hāl | Small, rounded pieces of ice that fall to earth, usually during thunderstorms.

harmonica

har • mon • i • ca | här mŏn´ ĭ kə | A small rectangular musical instrument containing one or more rows of metal reeds. It is played by blowing in and out through a set of holes.

harbor

har • bor | här´ bər | A sheltered place along a coast serving as a port for ships.

har • ness | här´ nĭs | A set of leather straps and metal pieces by which an ox is attached to a plow.

honeysuckle

hon • ey • suck • le | hŭn´ ē sŭk´ əl | A vine or shrub with yellowish, white, or pink flowers shaped like a tube. The flowers often have a very sweet smell.

hov • ered | hŭv´ ərd | or | hŏv´ ərd | Past participle of **hover:** To stay in one place in the air; to float or fly without moving much.

 in • fi • nite | ĭn´ fə nĭt | Having no limit or end.

in • spect | ĭn spĕkt´ | To look at or examine.

in • stru • ment | ĭn´ strə ment | A device for producing music.

Juan • i • ta | hwä **nē´** tə | Spanish equivalent of the English name *Joan*.

knap • sack | **năp´** săk´ | A leather bag made to be worn on the back. A knapsack is used to carry supplies.

knapsack

lav • en • der | **lăv´** ən dər | A plant with small, fragrant, purplish flowers. Oil from these flowers is used to make perfume.

lep • ro • sy | **lĕp´** rə sē | A disease that spreads over the skin.

lieu • ten • ant | lōō **ten´** ənt | An officer in the army, air force, or marine corps ranking below a captain.

lum • ber | **lŭm´** bər | To move or walk in a clumsy and often noisy manner.

maj • es • ty | **măj´** ĭ stē | The power and dignity of a king or queen.

lavender

man • goes | **măng´** gōz | Plural of **mango:** A tropical fruit with a smooth rind and sweet, juicy, yellow-orange flesh.

muf • fled | **mŭf´** əld | To be heard faintly.

mu • si • cian | myōō **zĭsh´** ən | One who is skilled in playing or composing music.

mys • te • ry | **mĭs´** tə rē | Anything that is not known or understood; a secret.

mangoes

ă pat	ĕ pet	îr fierce	oi oil	ŭ cut	ə ago,
ā pay	ē be	ŏ pot	ōō book	ûr fur	item,
âr care	ĭ pit	ō go	ōō boot	*th* the	pencil,
ä father	ī pie	ô paw,	yōō abuse	th thin	atom,
		for	ou out	hw which	circus
				zh vision	ər butter

night • in • gale | **nīt´** n gāl´ | or | **nī´** tĭng gāl´ | A brownish bird of Europe and Asia. It has a sweet song and often sings at night.

nightingale

now • a • days | **nou´** ə dāz´ | In the present times; in these days.

o•cean | **ō´** shən | The great mass of salt water that covers almost three quarters of the earth's surface.

on • ions | **ŭn´** yənz | Plural of **onion:** The rounded bulb of a plant widely grown as a vegetable. Onions have a strong smell.

onions

peered | pîrd | Past participle of **peer:** To look closely in order to see something clearly.

per • il • ous | **pĕr´** ə ləs | Dangerous.

pi • lot | **pī´** lət | 1. Someone who operates an aircraft or spacecraft. 2. An experienced person who steers large ships in and out of a harbor or through dangerous waters.

pin • chers | **pĭn´** chərz | Claws that can be used for grasping or squeezing. Lobsters, crabs, and some beetles have pinchers.

pin • cush • ion | **pĭn´** ko͞osh´ ən | A small, firm cushion or ball in which pins and needles are stuck when they are not being used.

pincushion

pi • rate | **pī´** rĭt | A person who robs ships at sea.

proph • et | **prŏf´** ĭt | In the Bible, one who spoke a message given to him by God.

psalm | säm | A song or poem that gives praise to God.

psal • ter • y | sôl´ tə rē | A stringed instrument used in Bible times, played by plucking the strings.

psaltery

R   **ram • parts** | răm´ pärtz | Plural of **rampart:** A wall of protection.

ra • tions | răsh´ ənz | or | rā´ shənz | Plural for **ration:** A fixed amount or portion of food for a person or animal.

ramparts

S   **Sav • ior** | sāv´ yər | Jesus Christ.

sea ur • chin | sē ûr´ chĭn | A round, soft-bodied sea animal covered with quill-like spikes.

sí | sē | The Spanish word for *yes.*

sol • emn | sŏl´ əm | Very serious and grave.

strange | strānj | 1. Not known before; not familiar. 2. Odd; unusual; different.

sea urchin

sug • ar | shŏŏg´ ər | A sweet substance that comes mainly from sugar cane or sugar beets.

T   **ta • co** | tä´ kō | A round, flat Mexican bread that is folded in half and stuffed with a filling such as meat or cheese.

ten • ta • cles | tĕn´ tə kəlz | Plural of **tentacle:** One of the thin flexible parts that extend from the body of an octopus, jellyfish, or other animal. Tentacles are used for grasping and moving.

ă pat		ĕ pet	
ā pay		ē be	
âr care		ĭ pit	
ä father		ī pie	
îr fierce		oi oil	
ŏ pot		ŏŏ book	
ō go		ŏŏ boot	
ô paw,		yŏŏ abuse	
for		ou out	
ŭ cut		ə ago,	
ûr fur		item,	
th the		pencil,	
th thin		atom,	
hw which		circus	
zh vision		ər butter	

tes • ti • mo • ny | tĕs´ tə mō´ nē | A public statement by a person about how God has blessed him

to • mor • row | tə mŏr´ ō | or | tə môr´ ō | The day after today.

trem • bly | trĕm´ blē | Characterized by shaking or shivering as from cold or fear.

va • cant | vā´ kənt | Empty.

vi • brate | vī´ brāt´ | To move or cause to move back and forth rapidly.

watch • tow • er | wŏch´ tou´ ər | A tower designed for observation.

weav • er | wē´ vər | One who makes cloth or other items by passing strands under and over other strands.

watchtower

wil • der • ness | wĭl´ dər nĭs | A wild place or region that is not lived in by people.

worm • ly | wŭrm´ lē | Feeling as low as a worm; sheepish.

wound | wo͞ond | An injury, especially when the skin is broken.

weaver

ă	pat	ĕ	pet	îr	fierce	oi	oil	ŭ	cut	ə	ago,
ā	pay	ē	be	ŏ	pot	o͝o	book	ûr	fur		item,
âr	care	ĭ	pit	ō	go	o͞o	boot	th	the		pencil,
ä	father	ī	pie	ô	paw,	yo͞o	abuse	th	thin		atom,
					for	ou	out	hw	which		circus
								zh	vision	ər	butter

Little Twigs

Morgan Reed Persun

In this fanciful play, a small beaver learns a big lesson. The play has three scenes, all at the same pond. A little stream runs through the pond. A family of beavers has built a small lodge and a dam on the pond. Use materials you can find easily to make a beaver dam and lodge. Then go along with Chester to see what he learns.

Cast

Narrator	Grandmother
Billy	Billy's father
Chester	Billy's mother
Grandfather	

Scene I

(Afternoon. A well-made beaver dam in a small pond. Two beaver cousins are playing.)

Narrator: Chester, the larger beaver cousin, tugged at a twig in the dam. It came out fast, and the beaver toppled over.

Chester: Five. That makes five for me. And what do you have? Only two.

Billy: Here's one! You'll have to give me extra points if I get this one.

Narrator: Billy, the smaller beaver, bit into a smooth sapling that was wedged into the dam. He pulled hard until his paws kicked up muddy water.

Chester: I'll have to help you. You're too little to work it loose.

Billy: No, no, you don't, Cousin. You just want to take my points!

Narrator: Suddenly Grandmother Beaver appeared on the top of the dam.

Grandmother: Here, now. What are you two doing?

Narrator: She tapped her tail on the logs and waited. The two beaver cousins looked down at their paws.

Grandmother: I see little sticks floating in the water, don't I? This is no game to be playing, pulling out sticks from the dam. Every piece is important; your father and grandfather know where every log and branch is. Do you want the dam to break and the lodge to fall in around our ears?

Narrator: The two beaver cousins shook their heads, but they did not look up. After a while, Grandmother went back inside.

Scene II

(Later in the afternoon. Same pond and beaver dam.)

Billy: What shall we do now?

Narrator: The cousin smiled a sideways smile.

Chester: Let's try to get that twig you were working on.

Billy: No! We can't!

Chester: Come on, you little twig-tail. It won't hurt anything.

Narrator: The smaller beaver did not like to have anyone make fun of his tail, which had not grown much yet. The other beaver splashed into the water and began to tug at the sapling. The little beaver thought a minute and then joined him.

They got to laughing and splashing so much that soon they had forgotten their Grandmother. Together they pulled the sapling until it wiggled. They pulled a little harder, and it began to give way.

Chester: Almost.

Narrator: Then a stream of water spurted out from beside the sapling.

Billy: Oh no!

Chester: Quick! Push it back in. Hurry!

Narrator: They struggled against the growing stream of water. The sapling seemed to have come out easier than it was going back in. The water ran over the little beaver until he thought he must have gone underwater altogether. And then suddenly the water stopped.

Chester: Got it! Whew.

Narrator: They both studied the dam. Everything looked safe again.

Chester: Don't tell anyone about this. Not if you know what's good for you!

Narrator: The little beaver nodded, his eyes still wide.

Scene III

(Inside the beaver lodge at dusk. The lights are low. In the background an almost inaudible murmur grows during the narration and thunders out before Billy's father speaks. It is gone by the time Billy's mother speaks.)

Narrator: That night the little beaver woke to a terrible sound. It was louder than any thunder he had ever heard. It was a roar, and it got louder. Billy's father rushed through the lodge.

Billy's father: Hurry! Get out! Get out!

Narrator: In the dark, Billy's mother found him and pulled him with her into the pond. In a moment, they were on the bank.

Billy's mother: It's all right. We're all here. We're all safe.

Narrator: But when the sun came up, things did not look all right. The beavers' lodge was a ruined pile of sticks. The stream swirled over and through it. The dam was gone. There was no more pond. Billy's father and grandfather went out into the stream and moved a few logs.

Grandfather: We'll have to start over.

Narrator: The little beaver stole a look at his cousin. His cousin whispered back to him,

Chester: Don't say a word! Not if you know what's good for you.

Narrator: All day the little beaver watched his father and grandfather pulling sticks and logs from the rubble. His heart felt heavier and heavier, until at sundown, it was so heavy he could hardly bear to breathe.

When his father came to the bank to rest that evening, the little beaver threw himself down by his father's side and cried.

Billy: I've done a terrible, terrible thing.

Narrator: And he told his father how he and his cousin had gone on pulling sticks from the dam, even after Grandmother had told them to stop.

Billy: We ruined the lodge. We did it, Papa.

Narrator: His father picked him up.

Billy's father: You did a bad thing not to listen to Grandmother. That was wrong.

Narrator: The little beaver snuffled and took in a gasping breath.

Billy's father: But you did not make the dam wash away. A flood from upstream came through. When that happens there is nothing that will save a dam or a lodge.

Billy: I didn't do it? Oh, Papa!

Narrator: Then Billy cried again. He was thankful he had done what was good for him. He had told his father the truth. His father kissed him and put him to bed on a nest of leaves. Billy slept peacefully all night.

Cousin Chester went to bed that night, too. But he stayed awake all night, moaning and tossing.

Chester: Ommmmmm.

Narrator: Chester did not know that telling the truth was good for him.